Money Wrapped in a Dream

by

Lucy B. Beutler

Published by
HarringtonGates; harringtongates.com
All rights reserved.
ISBN 0-9843836-3-8
© 2011

Dedicated to my children and grandchildren, who are keeping the *dream* alive.

2011

Acknowledgments

This book is part of a dream. My husband, Ivan, and I have been close friends with Jim and Connie Jenkins since graduate school days. We were young when we met, just starting out, but full of hope for the future. The years have grayed us on the outside, but on the inside our hearts are full of joy for the journey. We founded HarringtonGates with the hope of helping individuals and families use financial resources in ways that bring happiness. This book is a HarringtonGates product. Its development would not have been possible without the help, insight, and encouragement of the Jenkins.

My husband, Ivan, is the real finance man in our family. His faithfulness and steady hand have enabled my writing. He is my walking partner and reads all the first drafts. On the hills surrounding our home we have discussed the stories in this book at length, and I have returned after each session with new energy for the work.

It was most difficult to share what I was writing with my children. After years of correcting their English papers, I wondered how it would be to have them correct mine. But they have been wonderful, every bit as helpful and supportive as I tried to be.

I acknowledge my grandmother, who wrote of life with my grandfather so magically that it captured my attention, even as a girl; and my siblings, who have also written of my parents and our growing-up years in sensitive and remarkable ways.

A special thanks to Cassidy Wadsworth, whose careful editing added clarity and insight to the narrative.

Table of Contents

Introduction: A Shared Dream 1

Chapter 1: The Ledger 15

Chapter 2: The Gift 33

Chapter 3: The Battle 55

Chapter 4: Partners 75

Chapter 5: The Neighborhood 103

Chapter 6: The Hired Man 123

Chapter 7: Saying Good-bye... 147

Chapter 8: Building the Dream 171

Afterword: A Celebration Story 199

Postscript 1: Map of the Farm 210

Postscript 2: Who's Who in the Family 211

Introduction
A Shared Dream

Every great dream begins with a dreamer.

-Harriet Tubman

It was 1966, and graduation from high school was still highly fêted. My grandparents had given me complimentary graduation gifts—a crystal necklace and earring set and money for a new dress. I had used the money to buy some navy silk, which I made up in a classic sheath. The dress was much nicer than anything I usually wore. I knew my grandmothers meant it for college. This was the first personal gift I had ever received from them. Cash was scarce in our small community; even pennies were counted. Birthdays and Christmas were typically celebrated with verbal expressions of caring rather than with gifts. When I modeled the dress for them, complete with the jewelry, my grandparents' excitement over its loveliness pleased me. Tonight would be its first public viewing.

The party I was attending was in a city three hours north of the small farming community in which I lived. One of the fashionable hotels that opened onto the river was hosting the reception. My mother had been there once and assured me now that the mist from the falls hung in the air and chilled it, no matter the season. I would need a sweater. The afternoon sun streaming through my bedroom window made the thought of wearing a sweater seem ridiculous. It was early August, and the room was sweltering.

I hoped my date would not be a disappointment. It was a long drive to the reception and back, and it would be difficult to feign interest all that time. High school had been illuminating for me, as far as dating went. Some dates had ended awkwardly; I found myself wishing I had never come, wanting to say good night long before the evening was over. I was different than many of my friends, who tripped easily from one infatuation to the next. While I enjoyed the friendship of many young men, I hadn't felt the dream I carried in my heart spark with any of them. When I talked about the man my heart hoped for, my friends rolled their eyes and teased me. "Who could be attracted to someone like that? Do you plan to marry your father?" In the ensuing bewilderment, I had stopped airing my dream at all.

Tonight I was going out with a college man. That, in itself, was exciting. During the summer we had become friends. He was fun to be with, taller than I by several inches, with dark hair, a great tan, and a boyish smile. Though we had been raised in the same community, I didn't really know him. I was younger by several years, so I really only knew of him. But as his car turned in at the driveway of my home, I was hopeful. Glancing into the mirror for one last check, I was pleased by what I saw. The navy sheath looked unbelievable on my slender frame with the crystal jewelry sparkling light into my grey-green eyes and honey-brown hair.

The reception was charming. The hotel had been built on the banks of a magnificent, slow-running river, replete with waterfalls and walking paths, and we were drawn from the hotel out into the ambience of the setting. It was a beautiful summer evening. The starry profusion of the night sky sparkling on the water begged to be admired. We obliged for an hour or longer until suddenly we realized that we had indicated to my parents we would be home within the hour, and a long drive still loomed ahead of us. With no easy way to contact them, we were tense and uneasy.

It was awkward making small talk, trying to make the miles fly by faster and shorten the distance home. Earlier that evening, conversation had been easy. We had talked about college. I had dozens of questions, but we had pretty well exhausted them. There had to be something else we could talk about. Just before

Christmas, his father had suffered a heart attack. He was recovering, but the process was slow, and he was still unable to run the farm that supported the family. The illness had increased the worry and the workload substantially for everyone, especially my date's mother and younger siblings. When his father had become ill, he had been away at college but had driven home weekends to help out. This summer he had been living at home to help his father man the farm.

"I saw your father in church on Sunday," I opened. "He looks healthier, like he's been out in the sun again."

"It's good to have Dad out of bed. Most mornings he rides around the farm with me in the truck and supervises what I'm doing. He's not strong enough to work yet, but he does remember how things are to be done and makes sure I do too!"

"Sick farmers make poor patients," I replied, and we laughed together.

"You're right," he said. "They have no patience for anything."

"I'm glad he's getting better," I said and was genuinely so. I lived on a farm and could only imagine the hardship it would be for our family if my father were unable to work. "How's running the farm been this summer?"

"Hard, but better than it was during the school year when I came home weekends"

"How did you ever manage?

"It took some planning. I had to work like crazy to get my studying and exams done before Friday afternoon. I had to be home by six to milk."

"Who helped you?"

"My mom."

"You're kidding"

"Friday was game day. My brother was counting on me to be home to do the chores. Cows are fussy. They like to be milked at the same time every morning and every night. We depend on the milk check. Without Dad it's been really hard to keep the production up. I couldn't always get there on time, so my mom went out and got things started for me."

"Your mom worked in the barn?" I was surprised. I knew his mother. She was a hard worker but feminine to the core. I couldn't imagine her helping with the milking.

"She never did when my dad was well, but since December we've all had to sacrifice to keep things going. Mom's been great."

"Does she milk?"

"No, but she's learned how to bring the cows in for milking, feed them their grain, and clean up the barn when we're through. She'd skin me alive if she knew I'd told. Promise you won't breathe a word of it," he said, feigning an attempt to run off the road to silence me.

"I promise," I said, giggling as the car came back up over the shoulder of the road. "Why's it so important for your brother to play ball?" I asked. "With your father's illness, people would have understood if he quit the team. It would have simplified things for you and taken a lot of pressure off your mom."

He glanced my way, and I could tell he was trying to decide if he was going to tell it straight or just tease his way out of it.

Finally he said, "Because of the dream."

"What dream?"

"Since we've been little, my brothers and I have dreamed about playing high-school ball. I think it started with me. They were young when I made the team, but they were hyped for every game and came out and practiced with me."

"How did you find time to practice with all the farm work?"

"Basketball was play for us. You can always find time to play. I was their coach. Taught them the drills we learned at practice, told them about great players and what they sacrificed to be good at the game. It was a big deal when my brother made the team. We'd dreamed about that day."

"But you missed most of the games last winter. You didn't even get to see him play," I said quietly.

He seemed surprised that I had noticed his absence at the games. Taking his eyes from the road, he studied my face for a moment. Finally he said, "By the time I finished chores, most of the games I could get to were over. There was a lot of work that needed to be done in the barn, besides the milking. Getting to the games wasn't the most important thing."

"What do you mean? You'd dreamed about that."

"I had, but Dad's illness changed things. Every day my brother *had* to be the man at home. He couldn't be a boy anymore. The responsibility was too heavy for him. He needed to live a boy's dream. Playing on the team put hope back into him."

"Your coming home gave him that," I said softly.

"Yes," was all he said, but there was a smile in his voice. His decision had been a happy one.

Something about his goodness freed my heart. It wasn't the ecstatic spark I had anticipated. Rather, it was a swelling gladness, a joy that filled my whole being to know someone like him, someone who was that good. Despite genuine personal needs, he had placed those of his brother first. Finally I understood what I had never been able to share with my friends. My father had a heart like his. My dream was about sharing life with someone who had that kind of heart. I wanted my children to know that kind of caring.

The darkness inside the car was a gift as I wrestled with my feelings, trying to stuff the realization back inside. This was not the time or the place to share it.

The rest of the way home we talked at length about life and our hopes for it, laughing and enjoying each other's company. Before I knew it, we were home. Anxious not to further distress my parents, we walked quickly from the car to the porch.

"Thanks for a great adventure," I said as we walked up the steps.

"Not many girls get a moonlight stroll across the dam for a first date," he said. His response was full of humor, and we smiled together, remembering the magic of the evening.

After we said goodnight, he held the screen door open for me and then waited until I had gone inside before carefully easing it closed, holding the handle until the latch clicked and secured the door.

Smart, I thought. He was experienced with screen doors and didn't want it to clang shut and wake the whole house any more than I did.

Under cover of the darkened room, I stood by the window and watched him retreat down the front steps, get in his car and back quickly down the driveway toward the road. I wanted to remember all of tonight.

The lights were off, but my dad called to me as I walked across the carpet toward my parents' room.

"You're home?" he said.

"Yes, sorry to worry you. The trip took longer than we planned."

"Things go well?"

"Yes, we had a nice time."

"Thought so; I could hear you singing."

"Really, was I?"

"It's late," Dad chuckled. "Go to bed. Morning will come early."

"I will. Love you, Dad."

And so it began for us. I couldn't go to sleep immediately because I couldn't keep the music inside me; it kept bursting out and continues to do so today, over 40 years later. It was two years before we married, but our dream began on that long drive home. Through the years, our dream has transcended the cares of the world and given meaning to them. It is a romance we have shared with our children and hope they will share with theirs.

Forty years ago, I thought my dream was uniquely my own. Now I realize that the dream I carried in my heart had been nurtured there. It was similar to the one my parents shared, and their parents before them. In her journal, my grandmother wrote of my grandfather, "I married him because of what his letters revealed about the goodness of his heart." I was astonished when I read that passage. I knew my father had a good heart, but I didn't know it about my grandfather. Like my mother and my grandmother, I wanted to dream with a man whose heart was good. Most really good dreams don't originate with us. My dream didn't, and nor did my husband's. It originated from our parents, and their dream originated from their parents, and who knows how long the cycle had been spiraling before then.

Good hearts are not inherited. My dream didn't pass to me from the gene pool of my family, nor was it lectured into me or memorized from a chalkboard. It came much more obliquely, through everyday living with my parents and grandparents, as well as through the stories they told as we gathered around the dinner table or worked together in the house or the fields or traveled in the car. The indirectness of the approach allowed me latitude. I gave the stories credence because of what I saw in the lives of the people telling them. The stories were a source of nourishment and became, in later years, a mark against which I measured my life.

Dreams that have the power to bless generations are shaped upon a foundation of integrity, respect, vision, and enough financial resources to keep them afloat. Our dream required us to become people that we were not yet. We had to act, tweak, weep, forgive, and reshape our dream in the daily rub of living together. There is power when a good dream transcends generations.

Dreams we share as a couple can be powerful. Marriage is about doing something great together, something that may change the world. It is about accomplishing future things together, about creating and building a family. Executing such a dream can change the course of civilization, one child at a time, and one neighborhood at a time. In a limited sense, doing this is god-like. I call this vision a dream.

A dream about life and family always includes finance. It takes money to underwrite a dream. It is easy to spend our lives caught up in the frenzy and stress of getting. Without a dream that joins our efforts and shapes our vision, we may work all our lives and find at the end that all we have is stuff or disappointment.

Once a dream is in place, it defines a family's mission and reason for being. Everything else, such as income, budgets, saving, and debt, becomes a means to that end. While money remains in the dream, its importance is defined in terms of it. Thus the dream gives meaning to really important things, like saving and spending, and provides a shared vision and purpose during difficult times, of sacrifice, work, and waiting.

Money Wrapped in a Dream is a collection of eight stories about the dream my parents shared, the one I was welcomed into. As an educator, I began writing these stories because of the struggle my students had to integrate principles of personal finance into a family setting. There are many excellent personal finance texts. The principles are very clean and clear if there is only one person making financial decisions. However, within a marriage the alignment process is less straightforward. Something as simple as setting up a budget can become extremely problematic. Each of us brings to marriage the financial habits and traditions of our parents. Some of us bring habits of discussion and openness while others have never participated in a serious financial conversation, or they bring habits of dishonestly, manipulation, blaming, and tears.

Money in the family is about building dreams together. Many families need help getting started. Others need help staying in the dream together. Money Wrapped in a Dream reveals how one family answered financial questions such as: How do my spouse and I get on the same page about money? How do we build trust in our relationship where money is concerned? What do we do if there isn't enough money? How do we resolve financial conflict? What do we do when hard things come our way?

I also wrote these stories for my children. I felt it a tragedy that they had never known my parents as I knew them, as they teamed together to build a dream for us. These stories recreate events that shaped their dream. I have not tried to carefully analyze what was going on in other people's minds or even my own, but to share them directly, as I experienced them or as they were told to me. While the narrative is conjecture, and many of the details have been fictionalized, such as the names of the characters, the events in the stories are real, taken from personal experiences or from stories shared by my father, who in his later years was a ready storyteller. I am in them as one of the children, Mary. The stories take place on a family farm and are set against an agrarian backdrop that is disappearing from the American landscape; yet the challenges and feelings described in them continue with us, as constant as time.

We can't copy a dream. All of us have to do some things our parents never did and not do some things that our parents always did. These stories have been a great mentor to my husband and me. I was young when we married and new at dreaming with someone else. We had mostly wonderful togetherness, but we also had times when neither of us understood the other. Conflict and times of disappointment, selfishness (mostly mine) threatened the trust needed to keep our dream afloat. These stories provided points of discussion that allowed us to see ourselves through someone else's life, at times when it was too tender to discuss our own. They also gave me a lens to recognize moments we should celebrate. Most of our dream celebrations have not looked like Christmas or a birthday party; they have been much better. One such celebration has been included as the concluding chapter of this book.

Our dream was about the way we wanted to live together and what we hoped to do with our lives. We couldn't see our future any more clearly then than we can now. There continues to be uncertainty about what will happen. Our dream is a beacon that guides us, not in words or something that is necessarily written down. It is a feeling from my heart that rejoices when I get life right or is discouraged when I get it wrong.

Chapter One
The Ledger

Hold fast to dreams
For if dreams die
Life is a broken-winged bird
That cannot fly.

Hold fast to dreams
For when dreams go
Life is a barren field
Frozen with snow.

-Langston Hughes

It was cold that winter evening in 1956, outside and in. Dinner was served in silence. Ruth was tight-lipped and stiff as she washed and cleaned and chopped; everything she did was done with extra vigor. Her husband, Ben, had tried to cajole her out of the mood, but she avoided the outstretched arm he tried to wrap around her as she set the food on the table. The dream that had propelled them out of bed early that morning and for hundreds of mornings before was dangling like a crippled bird.

Leaving the dishes on the table, Ben drew her from the kitchen into his small office and pulled her onto his lap in front of the large desk. His desk was untidy; he preferred to use the desk drawers as decoration. If he put things in them he never seemed able to find them again. He preferred the "pile" method of organization. All the bills for the farm were on the left, and all the receipts and records of crop yields were on the right. It was December; the harvest was in for the year, yet the pile on the left was still sizeable compared to the one on the right. Despite the months of toil and sacrifice that year, they hadn't cleared the bills; nor was there money to live on.

"You've been looking at the ledger?" he opened.

"Yes—why didn't you tell me?" she burst out, refusing to meet his eyes. "Despite everything we've done to cut down and do without anything extra, we still owe money to your parents and almost everyone in town!"

"We'll find a way," Ben said. "I planned to talk to you about it, but I wanted to wait until I met with Father on Sunday. He may be willing to give us more time on our loan payment. Next year we could have a really good crop and pay off everything."

"Yes, or we could have another year like this one and lose the place and everything we've hoped for," she finished, still refusing to meet his eyes. "I can't bear asking your father for more money. He helped with the mortgage and went half with us to drain the fields. Your brothers already think we are getting special favors."

"Where's your faith," Ben queried? "You were raised on a farm; you know that there will be years like this one. We just have to cut back, see it through, and pray that next year will be better."

"We can't cut back any more. We've already surrendered every possible extra, and it hasn't made a difference," she replied decisively. "I can't live like this. When I go to town, I'm afraid to look anyone in the eye, for fear we owe them money. I feel guilty buying a few groceries."

"You're just imagining things. I promise that after I talk with Father, I'll talk to every single person we owe and let them know that we plan to pay after the first of the year. I'll have that part-time job in town until the farm work starts in the spring."

"I've looked at the numbers. It won't be enough. We'll need everything you make just to stay alive here."

"I think we can stretch it," Ben encouraged.

"Look at the numbers." There was toughness in Ruth's voice as she pointed to the columns in the ledger she had labored over during the day. "I'm going back to work. They need registered nurses at the hospital, and if I work three nights a week I could earn almost $500 a month. We could pay a little each month on these bills and some to your father; we could clear them by May. I don't think we have a choice."

The silence and disappointment that stretched between them was palpable.

Eleven years earlier, when Ben had surprised her by walking into the kitchen of her parents' home on Christmas Day, they had fallen into each other's arms. The war was over, and he was finally home. In the days and nights that followed they had promised to live life as one, finding little ways every day to make life sweeter for each other. What was happening now was not what they had planned; it was not in their dream. During the war they had spent four years of their married life apart. For almost three of those years he had been stationed stateside. They had at least seen each other on furloughs. But just weeks before the birth of their son, his unit had been shipped overseas. The last year had been especially hard and lonely for both of them.

Ben had returned on the *SS Walter Forward* as she made her last voyage home. The 300 men on board joked that she should have been called the *SS Walter Rearward* because of her lack of prowess against the strong ocean currents. Caught in the storm of the century, with wind and sleet and waves 30 feet high, the captain lost his bearings and sent a radar crew up to chart their location. Two minutes later they were back, running for the bridge, shouting, "Turn this boat around! Greenland is half a mile ahead." Luckily, the newspapers touted they had not run aground before they chugged back out to sea; chances for survival would have been minimal, as there were no other ships within 500 miles of them. Ben was a man of faith and never believed that "luck" could account for the many miracles that had brought him safely home. Through those long uncertain years he and Ruth had lived for each other's letters. The memory of what was waiting for him at home had kept him morally grounded through the debauchery of war.

Money Wrapped in a Dream

Even now Ben could remember, as if yesterday, his decision to give up his cushy clerk job at battalion headquarters. He was good at the work, a whiz on the keyboard of a typewriter. Ben enjoyed the perks associated with the position, such as no guard duty or KP and first break on all the good passes. But most importantly, for a man who desperately wanted to return home, it was the safest place in the army to sit out the war. The rub was the officer in charge of the section. He was the filthiest-mouthed man Ben had ever known. A constant barrage of crude stories and vulgar expectations compromised the office environment. For a married man who had promised to be faithful, Ben knew he had to get out.

His request to be transferred was granted. Incredulous, the Sergeant sent him forward, all the way to front line, from the safest job in the army to one of the most dangerous; but Ben loved it. He was as good with a rifle as he was with a typewriter. His assignment was to maintain telephone communication between the artillery and the infantry divisions. A team of five enlisted men and an officer strung telephone wire from large spindles mounted on the back of two Jeeps. In their forward position, they crossed streams and gullies, tacking the wire to trees and bushes in front of the foot soldiers and the armored vehicles. Most covert action occurred along the lines at night. Under cover of darkness, they delivered supplies and communicated with the forward observers. If a radio for one of the forward observers went out, Ben had to walk back to headquarters, get a replacement, and then find him again in the inky shadows and trade him out.

On Christmas Day, 1944, during the Battle of the Bulge, he was stringing wire over a mountain pass when he felt himself lifted into the air and then laid out flat at the side of the Jeep under the protection of the large spool of wire. A voice from an unknown source said, *Lay still, and you'll be all right.* A moment later the road around him started boiling up as shells from three American P-38s filled the road with chuckholes and craters. The driver of their Jeep was dead in the road, but Ben had been saved. Yes, he believed in miracles.

Their first son had been born and celebrated a birthday while Ben was in Germany. It galled him that soon after the birth Ruth had to return to work to supplement the $50 a month Ben received as a buck private. The second person he wanted to hold when he walked into the kitchen that Christmas Day was this little boy whom he had never seen. His small towheaded son was just waking from a nap when he peeked into his room. "Daddy," he called out with instant recognition and stretched up his little arms to be held.

That recognition had released a wellspring of emotion. Sobs shook his frame and tears coursed down his face, dripping onto and frightening the small lad he had pinned next to his heart. With reluctance, he had surrendered him to his mother, but the emotion of the moment left him weak and sobbing, unable to leave the shelter of the room, unable, for a time, to laugh and reminisce with other family members who were gathered in the kitchen. Ben had sat on the floor by the crib and wept openly and without restraint, his wife curled next to him, touching him, comforting him while their little son peered curiously up at them. Ben was weeping for what he had missed and what he had experienced, but he was home now, safely home; they were together in this small room. He could care for his family, shelter them, earn the bread, and Ruth could be where she longed to be, home raising this child and the others they hoped would follow.

He had grown up on a farm with a hard-working father and mother who taught him that the road to success was traveled by those who were not afraid of good, hard work. They had turned an unimproved homestead into a flourishing farm. With that upbringing, Ben had never been accused of being a slacker; hard work was his friend. After the war, he found a desk job and finished college, but he could not see himself working in an office forever with his family scrunched onto a city lot. He loved the land and wanted to farm. During the war, his father had helped three of his older brothers acquire good farms and begin to establish their families, but now that it was his turn to purchase one there simply wasn't anything for sale that he could afford, even with his father's backing. He finally decided to take a chance and purchase an 80-acre river-bottom farm that was mostly unproductive.

The neighbors thought he was crazy to do it, and they soon had supporting evidence. Shortly after the purchase, the river froze, forcing water into the sand hill on the east side of the river and causing a massive landslide that dammed the river. There was panic. Without the help of neighbors and friends from across the valley, who rushed to the river with teams of horses and equipment to cut a new channel for the river, the force of the built-up water would have washed away a good portion of Ben's newly purchased farm. After the slide, he vowed to Ruth that if she would help him he would make the farm productive and a nice place to live.

Despite the years of hard, hard work, their dream was still fragile. The water table was high, the soil filled with alkaline; it was swampy and uneven and most parts of it unproductive. Some areas were always wet and filled with clay that would have been better used for pottery. Even in the summer you couldn't drive a tractor across the farm without getting mired down. Ben did what he had seen his father do. He surveyed the land and leveled the fields and then, with the help of a backhoe, dug trenches and laid drain tile about 4 feet down so the groundwater would drain to the river. The land had dried to the point that much of it could be farmed. But that had not ended their challenges.

For weeks now he had worked day and night to claim his harvest. Heavy rain and early snows had slowed the process. The harvester and trucks got mired in the mud, causing long delays and crop losses as they worked to free the equipment from the bog. As the frost moved deeper into the ground, Ben had to wait until midmorning for the frost to leave the fields enough to allow the harvester to pull more than just the tops off the beets. On good days, he could work from mid-morning until early afternoon before the ground got too soft and the equipment sank into the mud. In the evening, after the temperature dropped and the soil firmed, they would be at it again, working until midnight or so when the ground froze and drove them from the field.

Throughout the harvest, Ruth had run a 24-hour food service from her kitchen, preparing food for the family and for the men who were working in the fields. She made hearty sandwiches, thick stews that could be drunk from a thermos and wrapped pieces of pie, cookies and slices of cake in napkins so they could be held in a work glove and eaten. The laundry had been enormous—heavy coveralls, jeans and jackets, work socks and long johns that all needed to be washed and somehow dried. The whole family had helped, the older ones in the fields, the younger ones delivering food, hanging out the laundry and caring for the babies.

Despite the fatigue and the worry, faith buoyed Ben up as they gathered for Thanksgiving. Over ten acres of sugar beets, a third of their cash crop, were still in the ground, and the freezing grip of winter was becoming permanent. Using sawhorses and sheets of plywood covered with Ruth's nice tablecloths, he had set tables everywhere to accommodate the family members who gathered to lend encouragement. Though cash was short, Ruth had worked a miracle and prepared a feast with their help and from what she had stored. As they gathered around the tables, his father offered their Thanksgiving prayer, noticeably long, full of faith and filled with gratitude, thanking the Lord for the beautiful earth, for land to grow food and feed their families, for their neighbors and the peace they enjoyed. Then he importuned the Lord to temper the elements that they might complete the harvest.

At the end of the feast each family member took their turn and expressed gratefulness. Ben had gone last. As he spoke Ruth had come from the kitchen and stood behind his chair, tears slipping from her eyes as her hand touched his shoulder and slid onto his chest, where he had held it gently in his.

"There will be enough," he had said, "and some to share. We have faith in a power greater than us. We have each other and a warm place to live, and we won't starve. So come on, put away those gloomy faces, and go have some fun." As if on cue, the children had sprung from the tables to play and celebrate the day.

Yet now, in early December, when harvest attempts were no longer possible, he had not claimed the harvest. About $2500 needed to pay bills was still stuck in the field, and there was no profit, no money to live on, and Ruth would leave today for her first day of work at the hospital. She was going to work to help pay the bills. Ben felt like a failure.

Too busy getting ready to leave to share lunch with him, Ruth changed into her starched white uniform while he fed the baby. "Wow, leaving me all ready," he teased as he carried his dishes to the sink and washed them, "Why so early? I thought your shift didn't start until three."

"You're right; it doesn't. But I think I need to leave at two so I can get my bearings before the nurses' briefing. It's been awhile since I've done this," she said, trying to sound casual, but he sensed her anxiety.

"You haven't forgotten," he reassured her, reaching out to pull her close, "You graduated top of your class."

"Don't touch me," she squealed, jumping away from him, trying to be playful. "You've got your coveralls on, and you'll get me all dirty." Despite the playful gesture, her words stung.

He focused on the dishes so she couldn't see the hurt in his eyes; he knew she hadn't meant to hurt him, but his heart was tender, breaking. It had never been part of their dream for her to work to support the family. That was his job. Only until the bills were paid, they kept telling each other. Despite the hard economic times his father and mother had experienced, his mother had never worked away from home, and neither had Ruth's.

"Anything you need help with," he finally choked out, avoiding her eyes and muffling his voice with the sound of the water.

"My hat," she brightened. "I can never get it back together after I've starched it."

He helped pin her nurse's hat together, centering the black velvet ribbon across the white front of the stiffly starched canvas and then anchoring it with her graduation pin. While he worked she reminded him of the chores and practicing the children should do when they got home from school and what they should fix for dinner.

Ben kissed her carefully and then picked up his work gloves and turned to leave.

"The baby's asleep, and if the school bus doesn't arrive before I leave, you'll need to come in and listen for him until the girls get here," she reminded.

He nodded and left.

Ben was fixing the fence in the calf pasture next to the road when Ruth backed the car out of the shed, drove slowly up the lane and then turned left onto the main road toward town. Intent on getting to the hospital, she hadn't seen him standing in the pasture waving his hat, smiling his broad smile, and throwing kisses with both hands. It was just as well; they had said their goodbyes at lunch. He rolled up the extra barbed wire and gathered his fencing tools while his shoulders shook and tears washed his ruddy face. Sobs burst from him into the stillness of the wintry afternoon air. Ben was glad no one was around, glad to weep out his disappointment in the privacy of the field.

It was close to midnight, and Ben was still awake, when he heard the car turn into the lane that night. He was lying on the couch in his night clothes with his eyes closed and the adventure book he had been reading laying open on his chest. It had been a long afternoon with plenty of time to think. Life wasn't giving them exactly what they had dreamed of. What were they going to do with what it gave them? This wasn't easy for Ruth either. How could she possibly manage their children and their home and still work three days a week at the hospital? How could he manage the farm and a side-job without her? He couldn't answer those questions, but of one thing he felt certain: if they didn't take care of each other, they wouldn't have any sweetness to celebrate when the bills were paid.

Perhaps it was the sound of her footsteps, heavy and tired as they came through the passageway and up the steps into the house, that helped him remember the early years of their marriage, how worn-out she'd been after a day at the hospital, how much her feet hurt, and how much she'd enjoyed the foot rubs he used to give her before he was called away to war.

Swinging his feet from the couch to the floor, he met her in the hallway. "Hey, honey, I've been waiting for you."

"What are you still doing up?" She asked, surprised but happy to see him.

"I couldn't go to bed without you," he replied honestly. "I did enough of that during the war."

She walked over and hugged him fiercely, her face clouding, tears brimming in her eyes. "I made it through," she said. "There were a couple times when

I nearly panicked because I couldn't remember what to do, but the worst part is my feet. They are *killing* me."

"I know," he smiled broadly. "You've come to the right guy. I know just what to do for you."

He rubbed her feet and legs until she finally relaxed. When he finished, they fell into each other's arms. Their dream had taken a turn neither of them had expected, but it was still alive.

***

When spring came, the ledger no longer showed red, and Mom was home again caring for us, except for two nights a month when she worked at the hospital to keep her credentials current as a hedge against hard times. With the spring, the earth came alive, and the dream was renewed. Dad loved to farm, to put the plow in the earth and see the dirt turn clean and ready with the promise of another harvest. Above the purr of the tractor we could hear Dad singing. Dad sang opera, love songs, foolery, and songs of faith. He was rarely in the house, but we could hear the music and sometimes see him in the fields, tired from the long hours of sitting on the tractor seat, standing as he steered the tractor through the fields and singing at full voice. As children, we knew the music was for our mom.

Dreams spring naturally from the hearts of children. There were many things we hoped for when we were growing up that were never realized, but we measured the quality of our lives in part by the sweetness of our parents' affection for one another. It made us rich.

Money Wrapped in a Dream

Author's Note & Discussion Questions

Our dreams take turns that we don't expect, giving rise to conflict and moments of coldness, silence, avoidance and disappointment. Someone has to break the ice. Sharing a dream tests our willingness to make the personal sacrifice to mend it. Sharing a dream also asks hard questions of us.

1. Ben and Ruth chose to meet their troubles head-on rather than hide from them. How did this happen?

2. How did Ben and Ruth "balance the budget"?

3. Ben and Ruth experienced feelings of anger and blame. What are some possible reasons that these feelings did not prevail?

4. This event posed a threat to the sweetness of the relationship between them. What did Ben and Ruth do to reclaim it?

Chapter Two
The Gift

Giving you everything,
I too, who once had nothing,
Am left with more than everything

-Robert Graves

"Would you like a chair by the dressing room?" the shop attendant inquired.

"No, this will be fine," Ray protested. The atmosphere inside the ladies' shop made him uncomfortable. He hardly dared raise his eyes as he stood by the mannequin from which they had slipped the dress his wife, Em, was trying on in the dressing room. He didn't like looking at the mock-up of women in fancy outfits, especially those displaying ladies' undergarments and stockings. Uncertain of where he should look or what he should do with his hands, he stood nervously, with his coat still buttoned up against the chill of the autumn weather outside, and rubbed the brim of the old bowler hat he held in his hands.

The clerk eyed Ray for several minutes. He was clean-shaven and well-built, with dark, wavy hair and deep-set eyes, probably in his late forties, and obviously very ill at ease. When he removed his hat she could tell he was not a desk clerk; he had the two-tone face of someone who spent a great deal of time wearing a hat in the sun. The fact that he was just standing there with his eyes darting about the shop made her nervous. Unlike his wife, who had made herself quickly at ease, pointing to several things she would like to try on, he simply stood there, looking nowhere in particular, waiting for her to return. Trying again, the clerk suggested, "Sir, you could wait on the chair by the window if you would like."

With a nod of thanks, Ray headed there, turning the chair slightly so that no one from the street would see him waiting. *Why am I so nervous?* he asked himself. Taking your wife shopping for a new dress was something men—well, other men—did all the time, but it was a first time for him. Em had been surprised when he'd parked outside the ladies' shop, and she had protested when he told her they should look inside and see if there was something she would like. There had never been money for the kind of luxuries that came from a shop like this. She had learned to sew her own clothes and most of what the children wore; the blue serge dress she was wearing was only a couple years old. What Ray really wanted to buy Em today was a new coat with a hat to match.

The white metal chair, with its curlicues, on which Ray sat was small and hard, a woman's chair. He was glad for the cushion on the seat but wished for an armrest and more padding on the back against which to lean. The chair kept him sitting carefully and unnaturally upright, with his legs neatly together. Maybe he should have taken one of the armchairs closer to the dressing room. He patted the breast pocket of his overcoat, feeling the outlines of his wallet, and pressed it against his chest for assurance. This was taking longer than he had envisioned. The whole process had taken longer than he had envisioned; but now his wallet was not empty.

When they had married, he had been almost 28 and she only 20, a city girl, blonde and blue-eyed, pert, saucy, filled with nonsense, with a waist he could span with his hands. Em had married him against her mother's wishes; even after all these years, Ray still remembered almost stumbling in on one of their disagreements. Arriving early to pick up Em, he had heard the sharpness of their exchange as it carried clearly through the open windows to the porch, where he stood about to announce his arrival.

"Em, where are you going?" her mother had queried.

"With Ray, of course. He's in town and should be here any minute. Oh Mother, don't you think he is just wonderful?" Em had enthused, making his heart leap.

"Em," her mother's voice was suddenly hard, "stop this foolishness! Haven't you heard a thing I've said? You don't know what you're doing. You know nothing about being a farmer's wife; you're not prepared for it."

"I'm not a child, Mother," Em responded. "I can work hard. You and dad haven't had it all that easy. You've had to work hard to make a home for us."

"Yes, Em, we have, but I've heard Ray talk. His land is not really even a farm yet. It's still a homestead. There are no buildings on it except a wooden granary he uses for storage and an old outhouse. Where will you live, in the granary with the harnesses and feedbags? What will you cook on? There's no plumbing, no water—do you know what that means? Every drop of water you need to wash dishes, to wash your face, to care for your children, to take a bath, to cook, you'll have to carry—and not only will you need to carry it, but you'll have to heat it. If you plan to drink it you'll have to strain it. Look around you, Em. Look at our home."

"Mother, you don't know Ray the way I do. He's a hard worker. We'll change things—"

"He may be a hard worker, but that won't stop you from becoming old and broken and worn out before your time. It makes me angry. Who does he think he is, asking this of you?"

"Mother, Father approves. He agrees with me. He thinks Ray is a good man," Em replied standing her ground.

"Your father is a man; he only sees the adventure of building a farm. Think of it, Em; who will help with your babies? I'm too far away; I won't be able to come," her mother continued.

Em was firm. "I'll miss you, Mother, and I'll wish you were closer, but Ray's not taking me to the end of the earth. I know Ray will care for me and our children."

"He'll bring you back in rags, and your children will be barefoot and without privileges," her mother fumed. Ray heard her sobbing through the open window.

"Mother…" there was a long pause, "we're not rushing into this. I know his heart. We're so happy. I know we'll have struggles, but we'll meet them together."

Em's voice had been sure, and that had comforted him, but the shock of what he had overheard had stunned Ray. For several minutes, he had stood frozen, unable to lift his hand to let his presence be known. Finally he had turned from the porch and left, knowing that he didn't have the courage to knock on the door.

Through the years, Em maintained that she had married Ray for what his letters revealed about the goodness in his heart. In the long months of their courtship, when he was away teaching school and working the homestead, they had corresponded by mail. Little by little, he had shared his boyhood. When Ray was 14, his father had gone to Australia to help his aunt and her children immigrate to America, leaving Ray and his younger brother to help their mother run the farm. He hadn't been able to attend high school while his father was gone, but when he returned, Ray had made up the course work and worked night shifts to pay tuition to attend the teacher academy. Five years later, he graduated. That certificate meant a great deal to him.

Ray had a gift for teaching and getting the kids on his side. Two years in a row he had replaced teachers whose discipline had failed. The boys in the upper grades were big kids, husky, some of them taller than Ray was, and not interested in learning. In one of the classes, they had run out three teachers in one year. The rumble on the streets was that they would oust Ray before the first week was over. The first day of class, Ray had walked into the room with his bullwhip whooshing, causing it to pop and spit. The students were familiar with a bullwhip and knew it could cut the hide out of an ox ear if the team needed discipline. Going directly to the front of the room, he had placed the whip above the chalkboard, where he could reach it easily with one hand. Halfway through the first class, he caught a spit wad from one of the big boys in his right eye. Without stopping the instruction, he picked up an inkwell from a desk in the front and threw it at the boy, hitting him in the side of the head and causing him to yelp in pain. The boy jumped out his seat and charged to the front, with two of his friends, to take Ray on. Reaching up, Ray grabbed the whip and started to slash it in their direction. The boys, seeing his intent, backed away and returned to their seats. Ray turned to the class and announced, "I'm here to teach school." Every day he brought the whip to class and carefully placed it in its place above the chalkboard, but except for the first day of class, he never had to use it.

It was the long talks with his mother that had planted the dream of a day like today in Ray's heart. While his father was away in Australia, each week Ray had driven the team to town to sell the family's wagonload of butter, eggs, and other farm produce. His mother sat on the spring seat next to him, and while he drove she told him stories about becoming a man. He had some of the best talks a boy ever had on those trips to town. On the way home his mother would review the accounts with him, and together they would consider what needed to be done to pay off the mortgage on the farm by the time his father returned. That had been their goal, and they had met it. His father had been mighty proud of them when he'd returned.

Still waiting in the ladies' shop, Ray smiled at the memory and patted his breast pocket again and felt the comforting outline of his wallet. Despite the restraint of being in a public place, he drew out the old leather bi-fold, opened it, and counted the bills. This was more cash than he had ever carried in his wallet. But today the money was secondary. The heavily embossed document that had been carefully folded with a single crease captured most of his attention.

Opening the document discreetly, he gazed at it for a long moment, savoring the feeling of immense satisfaction that spread throughout his whole being. Before the dress shop, they had stopped at the bank.

While he went in to deposit the check from the harvest, Em went down the street to leave a pair of shoes to be mended. Wanting to surprise her, Ray was glad she had an errand; the harvest check was enough to make the last payment on the mortgage. The heavily embossed document he held in his hands was the deed to the farm. The mortgage was paid off! They were out of debt! He could hardly believe it. Eighteen years earlier, in 1911, he had signed his name to purchase the sagebrush-covered sand hills that had become their home. Over that time, the mortgage had demanded every breath of energy and sucked up almost every dollar the farm produced. It had taken eighteen years to groom the land and turn it into one of the best-irrigated farms in the valley. Just a few hours ago, he had paid it off. He and Em now owned the 150 acres, free and clear.

With satisfaction came another flood of memories. After overhearing her mother's strong reservations about his suitability as a husband, it had taken real encouragement from Em before Ray had the courage to seek her hand. When Em said, "yes," he had vowed inwardly that he would not bring her back in rags and that their children would not be barefoot and without privileges; yet more often than he cared to remember over the last years, Em's mother had been right. During the first three years, the farm proceeds didn't even pay the taxes. Ray made $75 a month teaching school, and it was six years before the farm profits allowed him to retire from teaching and farm full-time.

The year their first baby was born, Ray was determined Em would have a new dress to wear when they went to visit her family and introduce their son. But when he brought in the harvest there had been no profit. He remembered the heaviness of the drive home, the plodding feet of the horses, the weight of the evening sky, and the stone-like shroud that settled upon him. After all the work, there was nothing to show for it, nothing to pay the taxes or the mortgage, and certainly nothing for a new dress. It had taken him a long time to put the horses away.

Em was wearing her go-to-town clothes when he entered their tiny home, and her face was flushed with aggravation. "Ray, where have you been?" she exclaimed. "I've been waiting for hours."

She punctuated the sentence by jabbing at the dying embers in the wood stove. "I didn't expect you to be gone nearly this long. You said it would only take a few of hours for them to thrash the grain and give you the money. You've been gone all day."

Her disappointment nearly choked him. What would she say when she really knew? he wondered. Turning aside, Ray began to soap his hands in the scrub basin. Everything had been ready hours ago; he could see it in the disorder around him. She had been waiting for him to take her shopping for the new dress; when he hadn't come she had undressed the baby and fixed supper without putting anything away. Signs of her irritation cluttered the small room.

Ray scrubbed and scrubbed, not having any idea how he would tell her. Finally he croaked out an opener: "I didn't get it."

"What do you mean, you didn't get it?" Em responded hastily. "How could they not pay you? Didn't they have time to thrash it? It's our wheat."

Turning from the basin, Ray faced her. "By the time I paid the expenses to have it headed and thrashed there wasn't anything left." There it was, out in the open. He had said it.

"What do you mean 'nothing left'?" Em asked in disbelief, sensing for the first time his deeply troubled nature. "Surely you mean there's nothing left after we pay the taxes and the mortgage and buy the dress."

"I wish I meant that, Em," he said, taking a step forward to touch her, to draw her to him, to close the space separating them. "There was nothing left after I paid the expenses of the harvest."

"Not enough for even some fabric? I could make the new dress," Em breathed, searching for a glimmer of hope.

"Nothing left."

When it was over, he wished she would have yelled and thrown things; that would have been better than the silence. But she didn't. She just withdrew, walked away from him, avoiding his touch, his look. Disappointment numbing her, stricken and white, she picked up the baby and then did something she had never done in their marriage; she closed the door to their room against him.

He spent the night alone in the cold silence of the kitchen, sprawled on the floor by the stove, using his coat for padding and Em's best tablecloth for warmth. In the night he heard the baby crying. He cried too and hoped his young son's cries would mask his own. In the early morning hours when he awoke, Em was there on the floor, curled at his side. He turned toward her and pulled her close, his heart bursting with the joy of her presence, the joy of Em in his life, the joy of Em beside him. He wept again, and this time she joined him. They sobbed out their disappointment together long and loud, and their weeping woke the baby.

That morning they were both a little worse for wear, neither of them having slept well. Circumstances had not changed. It would take all his teaching salary to pay the taxes and the mortgage; there would be nothing for a new dress this year. Ray watched as Em struggled to close the buttons on the side of her dress. Pregnancy had added some inches to her once-trim waist, and the five buttons didn't come close to meeting.

Em saw him watching and tried to cheer him. "Don't worry about it, Ray," she said, tying on her apron. "After breakfast this morning, I'll look through my sewing basket."

"What for," Ray asked? "You don't have enough fabric in there for a new dress."

"No, I don't have enough for a whole dress," Em agreed, "but I've got lots of scraps, and I think some of them may come close to matching the fabric of my dresses."

"What good does that do?" Ray puzzled.

"I'll cut open the seams on my dresses and use those scraps to add some gussets around the waistline; that way I can at least wear them with the buttons done up," Em finished with a grin.

In the end, the repairs were not as successful as they had hoped. Even with a man's untrained eye, the gussets jabbed at Ray; and there was no doubt that during their visit home her mother noticed them as well. Despite Ray's promises, Em had come home in scraps. And that was not all; they had lived in the granary with the harnesses and the feed sacks just as her mother had predicted.

Moving their home from the rented house in town to the granary on the homestead had been Em's idea. They had only lived there in the summer, but nonetheless it had been their home. During the school year they rented a place in town that was comfortable for Em and close to the school where he taught. But in the spring of the year, he left at the end of each school day to begin working the fields. This left Em alone, waiting night after night for him to make the long drive back to their place in town. One morning she had surprised him by announcing that all their things were packed and that she was moving out to the granary for the rest of the summer.

"Em, having you close will be nice, but it won't change the amount of work I have to do," Ray had protested, remembering her mother's prophecy.

"It will be fun, like a camp out," she had enthused. "Besides, you won't have to waste all that time driving back and forth every day." As she finished she drew him close, holding his face softly in her hands. "We can be together, and I can help you."

"You know the granary walls aren't finished to keep out the heat. There's not a single tree; the only shade is what's thrown by the barbed wire fence. Where will you cook?"

"I'll cook outside. We'll make do until you get time to add a lean-to onto the granary." Em had been emphatic.

Ray had loaded their things into the wagon and asked the landlord to keep their place until he returned in the fall to teach school. Through the years there had been 13 moves between town and the homestead, and they'd had three children before he quit teaching school, and built the farmhouse as their permanent home.

Em had been right; moving to the granary had allowed them to be together more. She helped him plant the garden and orchard, put in some shade trees, and expand the well so they had enough water. While they were working on the well, Em lost her wedding ring. Why on earth she was wearing the ring while she worked in the dirt he never understood, but she was a city girl, and he had forgotten to warn her. They had searched through the dirt for hours. When it got dark and she realized they were not going to find the ring, she had bawled her eyes out. It was so seldom that Em gave way to tears that Ray couldn't chide her; instead he tried to comfort her, telling her she was still his bride, that he'd always claim her and that a ring didn't mean anything. But it did to Em.

Only in the evenings did Em question her decision to move from town to the granary. Being alone in the granary in the evening was spooky to her, even with the baby. When it got dark outside and Ray was still in the field, her overactive imagination sometimes got the better of her; the shadows became real, and she would flee out into the fields to find him. One night he had been bunching the last of the hay when he heard her calling.

"Ray, where are you? Ray, answer me!"

"I'm over here," he had called back, "in the hay field!" He was at the far end of the hay field, about a half-mile from the house, and the only light was that of the night sky. His eyes had adjusted to the dimness, but Em was neither used to the dark nor familiar with the lay of the land, and the only way she could find him was by following the sound of his voice.

A few minutes later he had heard her again, her voice edged with exasperation. "Where is 'over here'? For Pete's sake, where are you? It's dark, and I just stumbled into the ditch. I've got the baby with me. Ray, where are you?" she yelled.

"I'm coming," he had hollered back, climbing up on Old Buck and heading across the field. "Keep calling so I can find you."

When he found her by the ditch in the wheat field, feelings of worry and then relief had tumbled out of Em. "I just got so anxious. You know those rough men we saw fixing the power lines this morning? I kept thinking they were looking in on me and the baby and they knew you weren't there to protect us." She had shuddered and wrapped herself around him. When she was calm, he had taken the baby and helped her up on Old Buck then handed up the baby and climbed up behind them. They had headed off toward home, Buck walking sedately for a change, as if he knew Ray's whole world was balanced precariously on his back.

Lost in his thoughts, Ray had almost forgotten he was waiting in a ladies' shop until Em emerged from the dressing room and interrupted his reverie. He saw clear frustration etched on her face. The red dress she modeled for him had a beautiful collar that framed her face, but the silhouette of the dress pulled tightly across her middle. With each of their children, she had lost more of her small waist and curvy shape. Pointing at the price tag, she gave him the "drop dead" sign, indicating it was too expensive to even consider.

"Don't buy a dress; buy a coat," he encouraged as the clerk rushed to bring a different style and return Em to the dressing room.

Ray's thoughts slid easily back to the past. When he had bought the 150 acres they were covered with sagebrush and all manner of brambles. Except for about ten acres around the granary, the land was too hilly for flood irrigation. Every spare minute, from early spring until late fall, he'd have the horses in the field scraping down the hills and filling in the gullies, and each step of the way he trudged behind them, filling and spilling, filling and spilling the scraper until a semblance of levelness took shape. Em teased that Ray had walked more than the distance from San Francisco to New York City leveling their farm. There were no engines or motorized implements to tame the land, only his strength and that of the horses.

Again Em emerged from the dressing room. This time she stood before him in a dress-length gray coat with good lines. The coat was made of a sturdy wool fabric and was practical, like the well-built shoes she was wearing, and wouldn't easily show the dust that seeped into every part of farm life. Ray looked at her and knew that if he had bought the coat last year this may have been the perfect one; but somehow today he wanted it to be different.

It had taken them four days to make their honeymoon trip to the homestead by horse and buggy. Each night they had stopped at the home of family or friends, who celebrated with them. They couldn't have been happier. He had almost forgotten that the buggy didn't have a top until ten miles from their destination, when the wind had begun to blow and heavy clouds assemble in threatening banks. It had begun to rain in gusts, sheets and pelting drops, and in no time they were soaked through. When they had finally arrived, she looked like a baby kitten that had just climbed out of a pond. What a sight! He would never forget Em as he saw her that day, 110 pounds of curvy young womanhood.

Now Ray had finally relaxed enough to look around the shop. He saw a plum-colored coat with a matching hat on a mannequin across the store from him. Leaving his chair, he walked across to the coat, lifted it from the mannequin and held it out to Em. When she saw him with the coat in his hands she looked astonished.

"We can't afford this, Ray. I don't need this kind of a coat," she breathed as he helped her slip it on. "The gray one is lovely."

Ignoring her protests, Ray fastened the buttons down the front and smoothed it across her shoulders while the sales clerk placed the matching felt cloche on her head.

When Em stepped back and caught her reflection in the mirror, a huge smile lit her face. She looked like a girl as she twirled in front of the mirror, swishing the coat this way and that, admiring the front and then the back and then the front again.

"It's perfect," Ray said to clerk. "I'll take the coat and the hat." Em stared in disbelief as Ray drew the bills from his wallet.

Despite living in the granary and their lack of stylish clothing, Em's mother had moved into Ray's camp through the years, allowing today's celebration not to be about her, but to be about them. Ray was glad for that. Their children had done a lot to soften his mother-in-law's heart. Honest and eager to learn, the kids had not gone without privileges, if hard work and responsibility could be called privileges. Working alongside them, Em had helped the long hours be fun. Each of them hoped to attend college. Paying off the mortgage would help with the expenses ahead.

While the clerk fussed over wrapping the hat and the coat, Ray drew Em away from the sales desk and into the shadows of the shop. Fumbling in his wallet, he handed her the embossed document with the single crease. "I've been waiting 18 years to buy a gift like this for my girl," he whispered.

Moving to the light, Em read the document. Quiet tears slipped down her cheeks. Reaching up, she held his face gently in her hands and then kissed him in public, full on the lips. They had sacrificed and worked together for this day, sustained by the power of their love. A flush of pleasure crept up Ray's body and illuminated his ruddy face. He was a reserved man who never did small-talk well, but today he could have shouted to the heavens. He had it all.

***

It was unusual in our small rural community for someone to dress the way my grandmother did. During my growing-up years she always wore a beautiful coat with a matching hat. She didn't get a new coat and hat every year but often enough that, in my young eyes, the old one was not completely worn out before she received the next. The gift never came at times you might suppose, like Christmas or on her birthday. Symbolically, Grandfather took her shopping in the fall of the year. On the way home from shopping, Grandmother would stop to show us her packages. Grandfather was shy about it, but I could tell he was pleased from the quiet smile that played around his mouth and eyes as he watched Grandmother open her gifts.

My grandfather dreamed of giving Grandmother a new dress their first year of marriage, but it wasn't until nearly two decades later, when he made the last payment on the farm, that he had enough cash to act on his dream. The beautiful coat with the matching hat was Grandfather's way to celebrate my grandmother, this remarkable woman whose love and loyalty and cheerful good humor made the hard work of his life meaningful and bearable. The coat was an adornment. My grandmother was the gift.

MONEY WRAPPED IN A DREAM

Author's Note & Discussion Questions

When a dream is shared, the money that wraps that dream is necessarily shared as well. Money and expensive gifts are perilous markers by which to judge the success of our dreams. Few dreams ever produce the resources that allow us to give the people we love all that we want to give them, especially when we are young.

In the story, Em's family does things differently, but she cleaves to Ray and the dream they are building. Consider the early years of their dream.

1. In what ways were they poor? In what ways were they rich?

2. Do all great gifts require a financial outlay?

3. What may have happened to their dream if Em would have stayed in the bedroom with the door closed all night?

4. What do you do when something hard happens in your relationship? Is it helpful?

Chapter Three
The Battle

In reading the lives of great men, I found that the first victory they won was over themselves...self-discipline with all of them came first.

-Harry S. Truman

The tarnished leaves of sunflowers, mixed with those of cattail, milkweed, and thistle rustled noisily along the barrow pits, and the morning breeze played them like a wind chime, sweeping up and down the gravel road and bringing forth majestic crescendos followed by tinkling autumn pianissimos. But Ben could hear none of the music. On the seat of the tractor, he closed the top buttons of his heavy jacket against the icy inroads of the wind; his thoughts were focused on a battle raging within.

This had been a four-a.m. morning. Despite his rolling carefully off the edge of the bed in an effort not to rouse Ruth, their old box springs had squawked loudly, waking her.

"Ben," Ruth had protested without opening her eyes, "it's still dark; you can't possibly get up now."

"Sorry," Ben whispered contritely, gathering his clothes from the back of the chair, "but I might as well get going, I can't sleep anymore."

"You can't see to do anything productive. Come back to bed for one more hour and then I'll get up with you," Ruth had pleaded, still unwilling to shift from her pillow and admit the day had begun.

Heading for the bedroom door, Ben had exhaled his distress into the air. "I've been stewing most of the night. There's a lot that needs to be done before the crew arrives. I've just got to stop worrying and go to work."

With effort, she sat up and protested loudly. "Ben, you didn't even kiss me hello."

Just beyond the door, Ben stopped and glanced back at her, a smile tugging at his lips. It was dark in their room, but the light in the hallway allowed him to see the shape of her sitting there against the pillows with her arms outstretched, waiting for his return. Walking back to the bed, he bent down and kissed her lightly. Unwilling to be so easily dismissed, Ruth wrapped her arms around him and pulled him down beside her. "Okay, so tell me," she whispered against his hair. "What is so pressing, and how can I help?"

Ben relaxed for a moment against the warmth of her. "You already have," he whispered back.

"I'm not getting up for an hour, but when I do, besides my usual 100 things, what do you need me to do?"

Ben shifted and sat on the edge of the bed. "Have Mary bring the truck to the field as soon as it's ready. It needs fuel, and she'll need to check the anti-freeze in the radiator and add some if it's below the line. The crew is going to be here at eight. I need her help on the harvester, so she should come ready to go to work."

"Okay, she'll get the truck to you, and she knows that you need her on the harvester. Why are you so anxious about all this?"

Words spilled from him. "In two weeks they're scheduled to dig our beets. If we're not ready, we'll lose our place on the rotation and be last again this year. You know what that means. The later we dig, the greater the likelihood we won't get them out of the field."

"Ben, that still gives you two weeks to harvest the potatoes."

"That's not much time; we'll need every minute of daylight. We can't afford to hire trucks and drivers to harvest the beets. I've got to be finished with the potatoes so our equipment can be reassigned." Ben rose from the bed and headed for the door. "When the crew arrives today I must be ready."

Ruth's question followed him. "Did you hire the same crew again this year?"

"Same crew," Ben admitted.

"Oh Ben, I thought you said that, except for Mary, the crew didn't pay attention and their carelessness caused a lot of problems. We paid almost double the wages last year and harvested fewer potatoes."

"I know," Ben admitted, "but how do I tell neighbor kids I don't have work for them? I'll take the tractor up to the field and get the potato harvester lubed. Have Mary bring my breakfast in the truck when she comes."

More than four hours had passed since then. At eight, when the crew arrived, Mary had not yet come with the truck. Frustrated, Ben unhitched the tractor from the vine beater and left the crew waiting while he went to see what was keeping her. Coming over the last rise on the road, Ben could see the farmyard clearly, and to his utter dismay, the truck was still parked there. Minutes later, the slam of the porch door announced his arrival just before he burst into the kitchen and exploded. "Where the hell is my help?"

Seeing Mary at the table eating her breakfast, he zeroed in. "I've got men in the field waiting for that truck, and you're still sitting at the table. What's going on? Why are you still here? I expected you an hour ago!"

Bewildered, Mary hesitated between finishing her food, which was a family rule, and jumping from the table as commanded.

Noting the hesitation, Ben ordered, "Get in that truck and drive it to the field, NOW!"

Mary, almost seventeen, sprang from her chair, took a wide berth around him, and ran out the door and into the yard without looking back. Almost in stride, he followed her, waiting only until she had opened the cab door of the truck, checked the lever that controlled the hydraulic lift, and started the engine before he leapt onto the tractor he'd left idling in the yard, gave it the throttle and roared onto the road ahead of her toward the field.

It took just a few minutes for the heavy farm truck with the steel bed to catch up with him and a few more for Mary, always cautious, to have the courage to pass him and get on her way. He raised his arm, urging her forward, past him toward the field. She didn't acknowledge him but kept her eyes rigid, fixed on the road ahead as the truck lumbered by. Ben was close enough to see her pretty face red and swollen from choking back the tears. Her tears caught at his heart, but just momentarily. Fathering was about discipline; someone had to maintain order. Discipline had been easier with men in the war years. They knew that no one was going to pamper them; if someone punished them, they'd better get over it and not sulk, or they would get it again. Mary had better get over it.

As the tractor made its way back to the field, Ben had plenty of time to stew over what had just happened. He had carefully outlined to Ruth what needed to be done. Why hadn't she sent Mary with the truck to the field sooner? Ruth knew the crew would be there at eight waiting to start and they couldn't do a blasted thing without that damned truck. He felt betrayed. It was nine; they had lost precious time, and he had been paying a crew for an hour to sit around and wait.

Why did he have to lose his temper to move anyone to action? Why hadn't Mary understood? What was she crying about? He punched the air with frustration. He was the one who had reason to wail. The very first day of the harvest, the crew all present and accounted for, and despite the groundwork, he hadn't been ready to start.

Why doesn't she get it? Am I the only person who knows that this must get done in two weeks? Ben railed to himself. *Am I the only person who recognizes what delays like this cost? Am I the only person who cares? I don't have time for this kind of holdup!* His inner voice was hot and loud now, and his breath scorched his throat.

It had been almost twenty years to the day since the landslide of 1947 had nearly submerged the river bottom farm before he had even claimed a single harvest. Ben had vowed to make those 80 acres flourish, yet despite the drains and the improvements, only part of the farm had been productive, and that portion was not enough to support his growing family. Seven years ago a neighboring dry farm of about 1000 acres had come up for sale; the land was cheap because it had never been productive. When Ben approached the banker about buying the farm, the man had been unwilling to loan the money. Though the land was cheap, there wasn't record of enough productivity to meet payments on a new loan. It wasn't until Ben had disclosed his plans to transfer the water from his 80 acres to the new property and put it under sprinkler irrigation that the banker bought the idea. In the arid country in which Ben farmed, water was gold. The right to a substantial flow of water that came with the original property turned out to be his most valuable asset.

What Ben hadn't known on closing day was that the banker's motivation to finance the purchase was less than forthright. A seven-year balloon clause had been written into the fine print of the contract that preempted the 30-year amortization. This clause required the balance due on the loan to be paid the seventh year. The banker knew Ben could never make that kind of payment and planned to get the farm back with the water attached. At the end of seven years, if it hadn't been for an emergency loan from his father they would have lost the entire farm.

Bringing the water up to the dry farm hadn't been the straightforward job he had envisioned. Despite his legal right to the water, the canal company was disgruntled that he was watering his land without paying for their services. It took courage for him to stand against men much older and more established in the community and put their legal harassments to rest.

Another difficulty was the high sand content in the creek water. The sand plugged the filter on the pump, and two expensive engines burned up, leaving the crops smoldering in the fields. Ben made a friend of the reclamation engineer who worked in town. Together they walked the creek and planned where to build the dam that would slow the flow and allow the sand from the water upstream to settle before it reached the pump. Stilling the water allowed him to pump nearly clear water from the top of the pond and permitted the sandy banks of the creek to vegetate and flower. It had taken some years, but now his fields were green, abundant and productive.

The well-groomed rows that almost disappeared over the horizon were a credit to his children. When he purchased the 1000 acres they were young and willing but lacked the strength and experience necessary to carry the heavy responsibility of the work. Now each of the older ones was better help than two hired men. He had struggled financially in the early years and would have been better off if he could have afforded to hire more help. But relying on the kids had brought the bonus he and Ruth had hoped for, the thrill of building the farm together. In the evenings, when he and Ruth could both break away, they would ride together across the farm, listening to the purr of the pump and dodging the spurting sprinkler heads, enjoying the field's lushness and a short break from the demands of the farm.

For a moment Ben's mind went back to the idyllic summer evenings before the pump, the sprinklers, and the endless fields. The evenings when he'd saddle up Buck, tie the canvas dam behind the saddle, lay his shovel across his lap and then ride to the house to pick up his two daughters—little Mary and her older sister, Susan—to play in the wildflower fields while he changed the water in the big ditch.

From the days of her first steps, Mary had been Ben's little shadow; she was his buddy. Toddling on her chubby legs, she would find him and offer bites from her half-eaten cookie or stretch out by his side on the floor and rumple the newspaper he was trying to read. From her sentry post on the porch step, Mary had always been the first to spot him. "Daddy, Daddy," she'd squeal as he rounded the corner of the barn, saddled and ready to go. Her shrieking brought Susan bursting through the back door to join in the welcome and the outing.

"Shush," Ben would hiss, "you know Buck won't stand close until you're quiet. Now stand on the top step and hold up your hands." Though this was a frequent evening ritual, Buck never adjusted to the melee and shied away, taking two or three passes before he would stand close enough to let them mount. The girls clasped their hands together and held them above their heads as high as they could reach. He would reach down from the saddle, grab their clasped hands and pull them up, one at a time, onto the horse.

"Horn, horn," Mary would squeal repeatedly, despite his shushing.

"No," Susan would counter, "you rode there last time; you're in the back. You always get your way; it's my turn to ride in front."

In the middle of the tussle, Ruth would call from the house, "Ben, don't let the girls get dirty. I've just bathed them."

After promising not to let them get *all* dirty, he would be off on his faithful steed, with the golden curls of his two small princesses bouncing to the rhythm of Buck's quick trot, and with their long dancing nightgowns, covered with sweaters to keep off the mosquitoes, billowing around them.

Though they never came back completely filthy, they were always bespeckled with mud and grass. While he tamped the canvas dam into place the girls squealed and danced, pretending to be fairies in the flowering grass. On the way home their sleepy heads rested against him, soft and trusting. Ruth would meet them on the porch, ready to carry the girls off to bed, curious about how he had produced this rapturous state in their rambunctious daughters. Ben smiled, marveling at the magic of being a dad.

Remembering this helped. By the time he reached the field, Ben's anger had cooled, but an inward anguish replaced it. With a surge of disgust, he wondered about what had just occurred. I'm doing this for the kids. *They're great kids, my best help,* Ben acknowledged, recalling the many times they had gone to bed after midnight or climbed from their beds in the wee hours of the morning to assist him.

He throttled the tractor back and swung into position to re-hitch the vine beater. With approval he noted that Mary had pulled the truck into position under the mouth of the harvester. The truck was finally ready to load. Over an hour earlier the crew had been ready to start. If the truck had been here earlier, it would be loaded and on the road to the cellar by now. The memory still chaffed. He backed the tractor into perfect alignment, carefully easing it into the position where he could lift the tongue, pull the beater forward a couple inches and secure it to the tractor with the hitch pin. Deep in thought, he jumped from the tractor to set the pin and collided with Mary. He hadn't seen her standing by the back wheel and had jumped right into her. Close though they were, she would not look at him. Instead, she threw a key into the dirt at his feet and, without a word, turned to walk away.

"Hey, what's that about?" he questioned, grabbing her arm and pulling her back toward him, trying to be playful.

"It's the key," she blurted defensively, still not looking at him. "I thought you'd need it."

Bending to pick up the small, golden key he recognized it immediately, and alarm bells began sounding in his head. A 500-gallon tank of fuel was kept in the yard at the home place for the refueling of equipment. This was the key to the tank. Each time it was used the tank was to be locked and the key hidden so trespassers couldn't help themselves. The missing key had been the cause of more than one farm fiasco.

"What are you doing with this?" he demanded, firming the grip on her arm.

"It's the gas pump key," Mary asserted.

"Yes," Ben cut in, his anger flaring, "and you know where this is supposed to be kept—'never in your pocket, never in the field'. It belongs under the rock next to the tank." He had rehearsed this point to the kids so many times it was disgusting. What was Mary thinking bringing it to the field and then throwing it into the dirt?

"Look at me," Ben insisted, waiting until Mary's tear-filled eyes met his, "What if your mother or one of your brothers needs fuel? There will be more delays today because of your carelessness!" He shook her by the shoulders to make his point.

"It was in *your* pocket," Mary blurted defiantly, not lowering her eyes, tears leaking once again onto her cheeks.

"What do you mean in my pocket?" Ben glared, not comprehending her meaning.

Gathering courage, Mary faced him squarely. "I was late because I couldn't find the key. It wasn't under the rock, and the truck was out of gas. I looked everywhere. I hunted for over an hour. Mom finally found it in the pocket of *your* coveralls." Pulling herself free, she ran for the privacy of the truck.

Her words stung. Ben had never seen Mary like this, hard and fierce. Fingering the small key, he watched her go. So it had come to this. He felt like a fool. Why was he so quick to blame the kids? Why did he lose his temper before he heard them out? She was turning away; a wedge was growing between them.

The crew was looking at him, waiting, curious. Collecting himself, he walked toward the harvester, calling them together for instructions.

"Look at the rocks in this field," he began. "They'll be hard to spot because they look like potatoes, but if you don't get the rocks off they'll go into the truck, and we'll have to sort the potatoes again before we sell them."

"I'm going to run the belts on the slowest speed," Ben continued, "and we're going to assign people to all five stations so that lots of eyes will have a chance to find them and throw them off before they get mixed in the truck with the potatoes. But running the belts that slowly will cause other problems. It will increase the probability that rocks will get stuck between the links and break the belts. Those delays are costly."

"The person on the viner," he persisted, "plays a critical role. I know it's the worst station. The potato vines and clods of dirt get to you before they're broken up on the chains. It's hard work, but you've got to stay at it and work your hardest. Remember what I've shown you: bend from the waist, and use your arms, not just your hands, to throw it off. Those behind you need a clear view of the rocks."

"Any questions?" Ben asked, looking around at the crew. "Okay, if you're clear, who wants to take the first shift on the viner?"

As if instantly frozen, the crew was silent, the normal talking and teasing stopped; not a single eye looked at him, and not a hand went up. This was not a new crew. They had felt the heat of his displeasure.

"Mary," Ben said, "you start on the viner. We'll change positions every two rounds of the field."

Well, that was that. He watched Mary as she woodenly took her place on the metal stand closest to the front of the harvester. She was the best worker in the crew. If they had any chance of getting this truck loaded in the next hour, it would be with her on the viner. Ben climbed onto the tractor, started the belts and lowered the teeth on the harvester, relieved to finally be moving through the field. They should have been digging hours ago.

They had completed their first round and were about a third of the way down another set of rows when he heard it—the loud bang and Mary's voice yelling for him to stop. Without even checking, he knew what happened; a rock had gotten into the chain. The belt was broken. Depending on where the break was, it could take up to an hour, maybe more, to fix, resulting in more waiting and watching from the crew. The frustration over yet another delay welled within Ben, boosting him from the tractor. As he swung down, he saw Mary standing as far away from him as she could on the small step near the viner, head down, steeling herself against the lash of words she knew was coming, refusing to meet his eyes.

Struggling to check himself, Ben did something he had never done before. He jumped from the tractor and began running, running across the field, running away, running as if his very existence depended on it, running to find time to think, running to stop the worrying, the confusion, and the frustration inside. He ran to check his tongue so he didn't say something else that hurt Mary, to try to sort it out. He ran across the large field far from the waiting crew. Ben had never liked to run, but now he felt almost weightless, the fury within speeding him on and on.

"Damn the deadlines, damn the bills!" he screamed at the sky. "I'm doing this for the kids!"

In time, Ben began to feel the weight of his heavy work shoes and coveralls dragging on his legs. His lungs were burning, and he slowed, gasping for breath. After what seemed forever, he began to circle back toward the harvester. A whole season's work was at stake; he had responsibilities. He had to fix the chain and get the harvester moving again. That was something he knew how to do, and that thought brought his only comfort. He couldn't sort the rest out just yet. Drawing closer, he became aware of the faces of the crew eyeing him in disbelief. Without saying a word, he motioned for Jim to bring the heavy toolbox from the cab of the truck. Together, they pushed it under the harvester, rolled under with it, and fixed the chain.

The first day proved to be a bugger: Two hours later the chain broke again—two links from the earlier break—sending him hurdling off across the field, his legs again churning out his anger. Shortly after lunch, a rock got stuck in one of the sprockets that held the belt onto the elevator shaft and broke it loose. After racing off across the field, he realized the repair couldn't be done in the field; he needed a part from town. The harvester had to be brought in from the field so the sprocket could be welded in place. It was three in the afternoon before they were back in the field, and by six, even with lights on the harvester, it was too dark to see the rocks.

As the season progressed, Ben continued to run across the field; it was the only way he knew to win the battle. Running became a pattern. Whenever there was a breakdown, he would jump from the tractor and race off, leaving the crew nearly as perplexed as they had been the first time it happened. Through time, the sense of hopelessness that attended his first runs began to be replaced with hope. It was easy to stoke his anger, but not lashing out began to lift his burden. Mary's polite distance was a poignant reminder of what was at stake. "I'm not willing to lose my kids. I'm not willing to lose my kids," he found himself repeating over and over as he ran. Somehow—don't ask him how—it would work out. He had to be content with that.

One night, quite by accident, Ben overheard Mary puzzling with her mother over his behavior as they cleared the supper dishes

"Mom, there's something wrong with Dad," Mary ventured.

"What do you mean?" Ruth questioned,

"Well, he's just not the same; I mean, he's different," Mary confided, hoping her mother had noticed the changes as well.

A little apprehensive about what she might learn, Ruth took her time. "What are you saying, Mary? In what ways is he not the same?

"Well, all through the harvest he's just been different. You know how angry he gets."

"Yes, I've seen him angry," Ruth acknowledged.

"Well, after he yelled at me for not having the truck in the field and made me feel so horrible, he hasn't yelled at me one time. He hasn't yelled at anyone," Mary continued.

"Really?" Ruth questioned. Mary had her mother's full attention

"Yes. I mean, it's weird. When we break down he jumps off the tractor and runs across the field, leaving us waiting there without a word. He doesn't yell at us or accuse us of being slackers like he used to do. He just takes off across the field. And there's nothing for us to do. We just hang around. Nobody knows what's going on. Sometimes it takes a long time for him to stop running and circle back. You know how worried he is about wasting time; well it doesn't seem to matter anymore."

From a distance, Ben could see Ruth's face as Mary made her report, and the smile that spread across it was a huge reward.

"Why do you think he's running across the field, Mary?" Ruth asked.

"I'm worried, Mom. I think he's sick," Mary finished

No, Ben thought, *I'm not sick; I'm just getting well!*

***

My father fought to change his nature. It took three weeks instead of the scheduled two to finish the potato harvest that year. By some miracle, the beet crew was between fields and willing to put us back on their schedule when we finished. As a family, we never really talked about what we experienced that fall, but something wonderful happened in our home and, most miraculously, within our hearts as a result of Dad's determination to be a better man. Nothing changed about farm life; it was still full of work, frustration and setbacks, pressures and bills, but there was more kindness and joy in our daily association. We were more open in our communication with each other, and there was more loyalty as we lived and worked together.

We dream of things we do not have, and our dreams require us to become the people we are not yet. In so many ways, at the end of the day, the real excitement in a good dream is who we are becoming.

Money Wrapped in a Dream

Author's Note & Discussion Questions

The biggest stumbling block to any dream is probably the dreamer. We are not yet who we must become if our dream is to succeed. Under stress we tend to see the task that needs to be done far more clearly than we do the faces in the dream.

1. In this story, what was Ben's dream? How did his behavior create dissonance with the dream?

2. Write down a time when you have seen the task more clearly than you have seen the people involved with it.

3. What can you do/what have you done to bring your behavior back into better alignment?

4. What did Ben do?

Chapter Four
Partners

> *The decision to kiss for the first time is the most crucial in any love story. It changes the relationship of two people much more strongly than even the final surrender; because this kiss already has within it that surrender.*
>
> -Emil Ludwig

The kitchen window was about the only thing on the farmhouse that had not changed. It had been almost twenty years since Ben and Ruth had bought the farm next to the river and started raising their family here. As the children came, they added onto the house and changed the configuration of the kitchen, but the window remained in its place, facing east and right above the sink. It was the lens on the world that Ruth consulted most often. The window filled early, most mornings, with the radiance of the sun. Ruth would pause from her work for a moment to watch the valley magically transform as sunlight painted the tops of the rolling hills, washing them with light and life.

In the morning light, the sagebrush was a beautiful sight, a silvery gray-green and brilliantly glowing. Watching carefully, she strained to see the mule deer that delicately jumped and played along the horizon next to the river. Only at daybreak could she hear the music of the bluebirds and the vividly yellow canaries before the heavy pant of the magpies and starlings silenced their song. It was this glimpse of the valley that she most loved. It held her motionless and appreciative of something few people heard or saw. She was an insider now. It had taken some years for her to discover the magic of the valley. These early-morning moments were her favorite, and the scenes that played outside her window were like old friends welcoming her to share their day.

Her alarm always rang early. It had been years since she had adjusted the setting. It simply went off out of habit; 5:30 a.m. was time to get up and be about the day. If she didn't rise early, the day would get away from her, and there wouldn't be time for the moment at the window or a minute in the sacred books that fed her soul. Raised on a fruit farm, where the best picking hours were before sunrise, Ruth was used to early rising. Many mornings before the buzzer rang she lay awake, organizing her day. This had been one of those mornings.

Ben was away. Leaving a 1,300-acre farm for even a day, especially in the busy summer season, was something he rarely did. It was a huge responsibility for the family while he was gone. Though the children willingly stepped up to help, the real weight of it fell to Ruth, especially big things like the worry over keeping the pump running and the pipe moving. Being late with water spelled disaster for young plants, and there was a quiet terror in her heart that the engine on the pump might fail under her watch. Of course Ben had left a number for the repairman, but what if the whole thing burned up? That had happened twice, but Ben had been home and made the tough decisions about how to proceed. Each night of his absence, Ruth wakened several times to see if she could hear the drone of the pump echoing through the valley. Thankfully, every time, the sound of the engine had lulled her back to sleep.

There was still a long list of jobs she wanted to accomplish before Ben got back. She smiled to herself, remembering. Deeply tanned and boyishly slim from the rigors of summer work, Ben, as a scoutmaster, had looked particularly handsome in scout-green as he'd swept the bed of the farm truck with short, brisk strokes. Ruth was a softy for this man in uniform. Just finished with hauling second-crop hay, the truck had been littered with hay leaves, bale hooks, and twine. He was trying to prepare the truck to carry scouts and equipment to summer camp. While he swept he talked, outlining information he needed her to remember in his absence.

"Don't forget that the sugar beets in the sandy part of the triangular field have to be watered twice; if you don't remember, they'll burn before the water gets back to them," Ben cautioned, sweeping the last debris into the yard.

He had already told her that, but in his anxiety over leaving, Ben was repeating himself. Ruth freed a hand from her packing and circled it on the paper. "What time are they expecting you?" she asked, tying the knapsack filled with clothes and sleeping gear onto the pack frame. Ben never knew before he left for a campout what she had tied onto his pack frame, but she rarely failed him.

"Over an hour ago," Ben groaned, heavy creases wrinkling his forehead. "I wish the troop could find another father to help out in the summer. It was like losing two men to let Jim go with the older boys yesterday; now I'm going, and they need our truck as well. It's almost the straw that breaks the camel's back. You'll have to get by with the pickup while I'm gone."

"That's impossible! I thought you were sending the truck back in the morning. I know you'll need it to bring the boys home after camp, but can't someone bring it down during the week and then take it back up Friday? Once you get there, you don't need it, and we will," Ruth protested pointedly.

In what seemed to be a seamless movement, Ben had jumped down, taken the pack from her hands, loaded it onto the truck, opened the door and climbed into the cab. "No one else is coming up. The only other leader took the older boys up yesterday. There's just the two of us."

Ruth had stared at him; he was one of the busiest men in the valley, and it seemed impossible that no one else could get away, that no other fathers, despite their talk and expectations, had anteed up. It was good for Ben to go with his son, for them to have leisure time together, and he was an excellent scoutmaster, not a soft-touch but someone who stretched, yet encouraged the boys. Still, it frustrated her.

Remembering the sandwich in her hand, Ruth gave it to him through the open window. "Just something to hold you till supper," she said, smiling. He blew her a kiss and with the next movement started backing the truck down the driveway.

Halfway onto the road, the truck stopped, and Ben's head popped out the side window. "Ruth," he yelled, "don't clean up any of my stuff, while I'm gone! Don't touch anything in the shed, and whatever you do, don't organize my desk!"

Ruth had smiled and waved him off, heading into the house. Ben would have to come inside if he wanted to make certain she'd received that message. Cleaning up was exactly what she planned to do.

That had been three days ago; he would be home tonight. Standing at the kitchen sink, she let the hot water run until the suds rose up like a thick meringue; then she started to wash the dishes she'd dirtied stirring up the bread that was rising in the pans and the cookies that were baking in the oven. In a few minutes it would be time to wake the children and start breakfast. Ruth soaked her hands in the clean, sudsy water. Washing dishes in a sink full of hot water that came straight from a tap was pure pleasure. She still thrilled at the luxury.

Twenty years ago, when they had bought the land, they had never seen the inside of the farmhouse before they took possession of the property. Though they had walked the fields several times, and she had pestered about seeing the house, no invitation was forthcoming from the owner. The house looked substantial enough from the outside, and in the end it wouldn't have changed things. They'd waited so long to find a farm that they'd have bought it anyway.

It was late on a March day when they'd arrived. Ben had borrowed his father's truck to haul their few pieces of furniture, and she had driven the car with their two-year-old in the backseat, wedged amongst their clothing, kitchen things and cleaning supplies. It had taken longer than they'd anticipated to finish their packing and say good-bye, and the gloom of the afternoon shadows had already begun to settle over the yard, but none of that had dampened Ruth's enthusiasm. Thrilled about finally having their own place, she had parked the car in the lane, rescued their protesting son from the backseat, and before Ben could join them, run quickly up the front steps, across the covered porch and, with great excitement, into the house.

She'd soon discovered that, though the house was littered with trash, it had five good-sized rooms: two bedrooms, a living room/dining room area separated by an archway, as well as a large kitchen with an outside entry. Compared to the granary Ben's parents had lived in as newlyweds, this was a castle.

Then Ruth had begun to hunt for the bathroom. Where was it? Surely it was somewhere and she was just missing it. Again she went back through the rooms, opening every door and peering closely into every closet. Suddenly, instead of jubilation, apprehension began to gnaw at her. Standing in the kitchen she walked over to the sink to turn on the water, but there was no faucet, only a sink. There was no water anywhere in the house, no indoor plumbing of any kind and not even a stove to boil water on when they found some. There was nothing to cook or clean with. The house lacked every kind of amenity, and it was filthy.

Disappointment settled over Ruth. She picked up their squalling toddler and sat down on an old crate that was lying in the corner. A towering grove of poplar trees blocked the light, making the house a little eerie. There was a peculiar odor that repulsed her, like something had died and never been buried. Ben discovered them sitting in the gloom.

"Ruth, what's wrong? Are you sick? Please don't be sick tonight. I'm so excited to be here, just us, just the three of us, just our family on our own. Finally our own place," he enthused, fairly dancing with excitement.

"Ben, there's no water in the house. Look at this place. There's nothing to cook or clean with, not even a corner free of dirt where I can put the baby down to play," Ruth pointed out, wanting to wail with her son.

Shocked at her appraisal, Ben looked around. "Are you sure there's no water? Look, there's a kitchen sink."

"Yes, but look at it; there's just a sink, no faucet," Ruth lamented.

"Well I'll be darned," Ben said, walking around the room and trying to digest what she had already discovered. "Well, there has to be water somewhere; I'll pipe it in. We'll add a bathroom," Ben assured, unwilling to be discouraged.

"I know we can change things, Ben, but what will we use for a bathroom tonight, and what about tomorrow? How will we live here if I can't cook or keep the baby clean?" Ruth continued, unconvinced. "Maybe we should spend some time with your parents while we make this place livable. They offered, you know."

"Not on your life, my fair lady. I'm through living with relatives," Ben responded, trying to be gallant and striking a ridiculous pose.

But despite his attempt at humor, Ruth sensed the steel behind his words. They'd been living with family since his return from World War II, over a year earlier, and though her parents had been wonderfully gracious, both she and Ben had longed for this day. He wasn't going anywhere, and she would have to make it through somehow.

"You sit there, my darling, and let your handsome prince come to your rescue," Ben persisted. "Your every wish is my command."

Ruth giggled; his clowning helped.

The first task she gave him was to discover the outhouse. Ben found it through some tall weeds on the north side of the house. With the shovel, he cleared the path then took the broom and brushed down the spiders before he showed her in. Acting on further directions, he swept out a corner of the kitchen, covered the floor with an old quilt and built a barrier around it with packing crates so they'd have a place for the baby to play out of harm's way.

Together they discovered the hand pump on the back porch that appeared to draw water from a well. Not wanting Ben to go off and leave her while he searched for the well, Ruth put the baby on her hip and joined him, combing through the tangle of weeds and garbage that surrounded the house. As they searched she was careful. The repugnant smell in the house was even stronger in the yard, seeming to hover in the air. Even Ben admitted to it. While Ruth wanted them to find the source of the smell, she didn't want to discover it. About 50 feet from the house, they tripped across a large circular piece of iron with a handle that looked like a lid. Dragging it off into the weeds, they discovered that beneath the spherical covering was a well. Ben was exultant, but Ruth gagged, and the baby cried at her side; the terrible odor was exuding from the shaft.

"Its sulfur," Ben exclaimed. "Rotten egg gas, that's what we can smell. I should have suspected as much with hot springs up the road."

"Watch," he admonished, striking a match on the side of the shaft and dropping it into the well. A bright blue flame popped loudly in the air, followed by a suffocating cloud of white smoke.

"Ben, what does this mean?" Ruth sputtered, turning away. "Does our drinking water come from here?"

"I think so," Ben admitted. "I think this well provides all the water for the house."

"Will it taste like it smells?" Ruth questioned.

For the first time since they had arrived, Ben sobered. "Possibly," he admitted. "There's a good chance it might."

They stood together in stunned silence, looking at the house and then back at the well, trying to comprehend it all. Confused and hungry, the baby continued to wail. Thank heavens Ruth's mother had fixed them a large picnic basket full of food. After what they had just discovered, all of them needed a pick-me-up. Finding some lye soap and a basin that would hold water, they washed on the porch then went inside, crawled over the barricade Ben had made for the baby and sat down on the blanket next to him in their one clean space. When she opened the basket, Ruth found that her mother had packed all of her favorites: fried chicken, homemade rolls and potato salad, with a bottle of canned peaches and a frosted two-layer chocolate cake that had somehow survived the trip perfectly. How had her mother known that they would need the comfort of a good meal? That was a lesson Ruth never forgot.

Content, the baby fell asleep in his little pen after dinner while Ruth and Ben continued to work into the night, hauling out the garbage, sweeping the house, floors, walls and ceilings and mopping them down with water from the pump. It was cold water, but she added plenty of her mother's lye soap to stiffen it. With the windows open, the kitchen dried enough for them to roll out their quilts on the floor and make a bed for the night.

Ruth got into bed first; she'd washed up in the basin Ben had positioned by the pump, complete with a string to hang their towel on. "Don't turn the light off," she cautioned nervously as he closed the kitchen door and walked over to pull the string on the bulb hanging from the ceiling.

"Why?" Ben asked. "I can't sleep with the lights on."

"Well tonight I can't sleep with them off! You saw all the mouse droppings we swept up. We're sleeping on the floor, and as soon as it's dark the mice will run all over us," Ruth insisted.

Ben felt the steel in her voice and knew it was no use to try to convince her otherwise. Leaving the light burning, he crawled in next to her and pulled her close, cradling her head on his arm.

His touch released the tears she'd held at bay since their discoveries earlier in the afternoon. She cried in great gasping gulps until there was nothing left.

"It will be better in the morning; you'll see," Ben had assured her over and over again, trying to comfort her. "Everything is better in the morning."

And it was.

Even twenty years later, Ben and Ruth were still learning how to dream together. He was helping her see beyond daily disappointments and focus on what they were building. She was a levelheaded realist and quickly saw the bottom line, which was valuable in their relationship but sometimes discouraging. She loved to work and gave evidence of her love through the things her hands accomplished. Ben brought words, music, poetry, and some silliness to their lives. It was Ben's good heart, along with his hopefulness and inner buoyancy that had drawn Ruth to him.

He would be home today. Opening the kitchen window, Ruth listened intently for the drone of the pump and after some minutes heard it chugging away; the sound was like music. With relief, she turned back to the griddle and began flipping pancakes. She had taken a few minutes to put on a cheerful tablecloth and the glass tumblers reserved for special occasions. Usually breakfast required expediency and a meal with staying power like whole-wheat mush or fried eggs and potatoes with toast on the side, but this morning they were having pancakes. The children had all worked cheerfully while Ben was gone, and before they went out to finish their chores, they would celebrate. Since moving to the farmhouse, there had been many festivities around this table and at other places on the farm. It was surprising how different those occasions had been from the birthday parties and anniversaries Ruth had initially envisioned.

They had celebrated the bathroom just a few days before their second baby was born. Rainy days were the only time Ben could leave work in the field to plumb the room; Ruth had prayed for rainy days. The mice they had suspected their first night in the farmhouse turned out to be river rats that foraged on the dead fish trapped in holes around the roots of the big poplar trees when the river flooded out of its banks during the winter. One by one, and as time permitted, Ben felled the big trees, and the rats left the yard. Each downing was celebrated with a huge bonfire from the wood of the tree and a hot dog roast with marshmallows for a topper. The water from the well was not only full of sulfur, but it was full of mineral as well, which turned their white clothes brown and was nasty to drink. When her parents came to visit they brought their own water; when they had company, Ruth served Kool-Aid or bottled homemade root beer so they didn't have to drink the water. They dug two other wells, but there was no improvement in the quality of the water.

Fourteen years after their move into the farmhouse, Ben devised a scheme to get culinary water from a spring he owned on the east side of the river into the farmhouse. The plan involved a mile and a half of steel pipe that ran down the hill from the spring to the river, under the river and across the fields to the farmhouse. With a backhoe, Ben dug the trenches and connected the pipe on both sides of the river before facing the challenge of linking the two lines underwater.

Early in December the power company agreed not to generate electricity during the afternoon hours, to accommodate the project. Working in hip waders with his brothers, Ben drove the backhoe out into the river. The water was icy, but only about two feet deep, and they made good time digging a trench deep enough to cover the pipe and protect it from the current. However, laying the pipe and connecting the threads underwater was another story.

Attaching one end of a heavy chain to the backhoe and threading the other end through the pipe, Ben sat on the pipe and forced it underwater, into the trench. One of his brothers worked the other end of the chain, trying to get the two ends of the pipe close enough to screw them together. Things were going well, and they were just preparing to connect the last pipe, when a wall of water came rushing down the river channel right at them. Someone at the power company had forgotten the agreement. His brothers noticed the water was rising rapidly and raised the alarm in time to get the equipment and all workers safely to shore. All except Ben, who had remained in the freezing water. Desperate to finish the line, he worked underwater to insure that the joint was coupled properly. When they dragged him out, he was half-frozen and half-drowned.

Waiting in the house, Ruth had been anxious. Early that morning she had filled every large container they owned with water, to get them through the day. They had to shut off the water to the house to connect the new line. During the morning she'd sent sandwiches and hot soup to the men at the river to warm them. But just minutes ago, their oldest son, Mark, had raced into the house to report that the river had risen and that Ben was trapped in the frigid water.

Instinctively, she knew they needed a bathtub full of warm water. With water to the house shut off, the only way to heat it was on the stove. She emptied water from the buckets into the four largest pots and turned the burners on high, hoping the electric range didn't blow a fuse.

Ben was barely lucid, and blue with cold, when they got him to the house and into the tub. For the next two hours, except for quick trips to the stove for more hot water, Ruth knelt by the tub. She mixed the heated water with cool water and poured it as continuously as possible over his frozen limbs, encouraging and caressing him with her voice. Finally, the shakes began, and pink began to fight the blue from his skin.

Suddenly, almost convulsively, Ben sat up and started throwing off the hot towels and washcloths she had placed on his body for warmth. "Okay, get me out of here," he demanded.

"No Ben, what are you thinking? Lie back down—you're still half frozen," Ruth ordered, relieved but alarmed, pushing him back into the water. "You've got to stay in this tub until your body has normalized."

"I'm as normal as I'm going to get," Ben insisted, gathering himself again and trying to sit up. "I'm not lying in this bathtub a minute longer. I've got to find out about the pipe."

Pushing him down again, Ruth asked, "Find out what about the pipe? Mark said you finished the last joint just before the water rose."

"I think I felt the coupling turn into place as the water hit me," Ben said through chattering teeth, "but it could have just been the force of the water spinning it." He was shaking badly, which was a good sign.

"How will you know?" Ruth asked, laying the hot towels on his stomach and chest again. "Will you have to go back to the river?"

"If it isn't connected, I'll have to go back," Ben answered, trying again to rise.

Alarmed, Ruth pushed him down again. "Ben, stop this nonsense; surely not today. Rest and warm up; get your feet under you. Two hours ago you were almost dead."

"If the coupling didn't latch I'll have to go back. You'll send me back. We've invested too much money and time. I've got to make good on this!" Ben said angrily.

"I know you do," Ruth said, trying to soothe him. "We've waited a long time for good water; we can wait a little longer."

"Help me get dressed." Ben was emphatic, sitting upright. "Wrap me in some quilts. I've got to find out!"

He was shaking from head to toe but immovable as she tried to push him back down into the water. Realizing she was fighting a losing battle, she stood behind him in the water and helped him stand. "Can you tell from the house?"

"From the water," Ben gasped, his voice trembling. "No pressure…Dirty water…"

Half an hour later the family had gathered together around the kitchen sink. Ben sat with his feet on the step of a high stool, dressed in heavy flannel pajamas, a thick robe, three pairs of wool socks, and a stocking cap. Following his father's instructions, Mark inched his way through the crawl space under the house and used a crescent wrench to open the water valve to the house. When he tapped with the wrench, announcing that he had been successful, Ben turned the handle and opened the faucet. As the air in the line escaped, the water spit and jerked out of the tap and then began to run dirty and brown. The faces in the group were anxious.

"Don't worry," Ben said. "This water has been sitting in the pipes all day. It's what comes later that will tell the story."

They hung around, watching the faucet like a picture show; the water ran brown, brown, and brown. Every so often Ruth dipped out a glassful of water and set it on the window ledge to act as a comparison. After a time they began to wonder if it was clearing or if they had just gotten used to the color, but gradually the color began to change; slowly but surely, they all agreed, it was getting clearer. They began to laugh and cheer, but Ben was cautious. "Wait," he admonished, "wait for 15 more minutes before we celebrate." The time ticked by slowly, but the water remained clear. When the timer went off, cheering erupted in the room. There was hugging, and they began to dance and shout. It was like New Year's, except better. Ruth served their refreshments, not cake with candles or ice cream, but something even better: large glasses of crystal-clear spring water straight from their very own tap.

Leaning on the rake now, Ruth could hear the droning of the pump. She surveyed with pleasure the grounds around their home. It would never rival the large white Victorian with the green roof and sunroom in which she had been raised. Surrounded by stately Douglas firs and her mother's flowers, her girlhood home had looked like a storybook house. The soil here was brackish. Most of the trees and flowers they'd planted had died before they ever took root. The only trees that had survived were Russian Olives and poplars, which her father didn't consider to be proper trees. Today, though, Ruth was proud of their home.

While Ben was away, she and the children had used every spare minute to spruce up the yard. They mowed the grass around the house, along the ditch banks in front of the house, under the currant bushes, and around the wild roses. Then they tackled the yard, the corrals, and the outbuildings where Ben parked farm equipment and kept his abundant collection of "spare parts" which he used to repair equipment and fences around the place. They pulled the weeds, organized the parts, picked up tools, and hauled debris to the dump. For the first time in a long while, they parked the car in the garage. It took many trips with the pickup to haul it all out. When Ben returned today he would find the yard, the garage, his tool shed and his desk, raked, clipped, pruned and neat.

Ben would be upset. She had done exactly what he had asked her not to do: clean up things in all of his revered spaces. He always planned to get organized, clean up the yard and put his tools back where they came from, but he never found the time. Constantly undercapitalized, he would be drawn away by something more pressing. Organization was not necessary for Ben's world; he knew where most things were—but he was the only one. It was almost impossible for anyone else to find things in the tool shed or in the garage. Nothing was on the shelf, and bits of leftovers from repairs were scattered about. The idea of storing the car or the truck in the garage was ridiculous. He was a genius with the welder and had saved them thousands of dollars by fixing and improvising farm equipment himself, but the remains of each project were still in the yard—extra wheels, barrels, pipes and angle iron—all with a healthy crop of weeds growing up through them. Ben loved to stop at army surplus yards to see what was new, many times returning with a replica of something he already had but couldn't find in the weeds.

The disorganization was unsightly and fostered hard feelings between Ben and Ruth. When Ben sent one of the children to get something from the shed, they rarely could find it and came to the house to solicit her aid. Some hours later they usually discovered it, but the delays and miscommunication resulted in irritation and frustration. Ruth had adjusted her dream from the large Victorian to their sturdy farmhouse by the river, but she visualized the place neat, clean, and well-groomed—not an up-and-coming salvage yard.

It was chore time when Ben, with their son Jim beside him, pulled the farm truck into the yard. Ruth and the children came from every corner, jumping about with shouts of welcome, everyone talking at once. Ben stepped out of the truck and cocked his head to listen for the pump. Hearing the familiar drone, he let the lines around his mouth relax into a smile, and he gave her a whiskery kiss. Jim wanted everyone to see his treasures and listen to his tales, but he was outnumbered. He had to listen to the others recount all that had happened at home while they were gone, especially the trips they'd made to the junkyard. While they jabbered, Ben craned his neck, looking this way and that around the place. Finally he picked up his scout case and headed for the house. Ruth knew he was headed for his office and began to fear she had gone too far by cleaning his desk.

He was quiet at supper, giving Jim plenty of space to spin his stories without any reframing. As the family finished, he looked around at them and announced, "You kids do the dishes; I'm going to take your mother for a drive and check things out around the farm." There were the usual protests, but Ben didn't hear any of them.

Grabbing her jacket, Ruth followed him out into the yard. As many times as she had justified what she would say at this moment, she dreaded the confrontation. He glanced around the yard, trying to find the pickup, and was irritated when he found it parked neatly in the shed. She could tell that not being able to find his truck was close to the last straw.

Inside the truck, Ben's frustration was evident. He yanked on the bar to adjust the seat and took elaborate pains to adjust the mirror. Then, noticing the stack of yellow receipts from the junkyard on the dash, he fingered them and said, "Looks like you worked the pickup out pretty hard while I was gone."

"It took several loads to get it all cleaned up," she submitted, working to keep the conversation safe. "You would have been proud of the kids; they worked really hard."

"You don't have any idea what is valuable, Ruth." Ben's words flew at her. "I'm going to have to buy most of the stuff back, and what about the farm papers you moved—what happens if I never find those?"

"If you want to keep them, put them on a shelf or in a drawer," she flung back. "There seems to be plenty of space there."

The silence between them was stiff and accusing. Finally, turning on the seat to face her, Ben started again.

"Ruth, I'm trying to understand this; didn't you hear what I asked when I left for camp?"

Ruth took some time to respond, but when she did her voice was level and firm, and though she had considered rationalizing deafness, in the end she told the truth. "Yes, I heard you."

"What did I ask?" Ben queried.

"You asked me not to clean up any of your stuff, especially your stuff in the shed, and not to organize your desk."

"I don't understand; you heard, but you did it anyway. Why? That's my space; those were my things."

"I did it, Ben, because you haven't heard me." Ruth's voice was level.

"What do you mean, I haven't heard you?" Ben asked, surprised at her turn of the table.

"We've lived here for almost 20 years, and all that time you've promised to clean up the yard and make our house look respectable, but you never have," Ruth replied.

"What are you saying?" Ben flared. "Are you calling me a sloth?"

"No," she said. "I'm just telling the truth of it."

"What are you asking of me?" Ben blurted, his voice filled with exasperation. "I'm swamped. We've got two farms, and it requires everything I've got to make them pay."

"I know you're busy, Ben," she said solicitously. "I'm not asking for money. I'm busy too. I don't get in bed any sooner than you do, but this dream to build our place and launch our children only works if it's our dream, not just your dream. You haven't heard me. I'm through living in a place that looks like a salvage yard." She finished, but not before Ben saw the fire in her eyes.

"I know this place doesn't look like what you've envisioned," he responded apologetically. "We've had to put off that part of the dream. In a couple years we'll build the new house; we'll fix up the yard then."

"No, Ben, I'm not waiting for sometime later or a new house," Ruth went on. "In the morning look around and just see how lovely our place is when the grass is cut, the weeds are pulled and things are organized and neat. It almost took my breath away when we finished today."

"I don't like you sorting my stuff," Ben said defensively, trying to bring the conversation back to his side of the table.

"I promise not to touch anything that's on a shelf."

They sat together in the truck, looking at each other. After what seemed forever, Ben took her hand, squeezed it, put it on his leg where he could hold it with the hand he didn't need for driving, and started the pickup down the road. Ruth snuggled next to him on the seat and whispered softly into his ear his own words of comfort. "It will look better in the morning, Ben; it always does."

***

In their shared dream, my parents played different roles. Through the years they discovered each other's strengths and weaknesses. My father was the instigator of great ideas and the big-picture man. My mother kept his feet on the ground, managed the details, and kept the order that allowed them to stay afloat.

As much as my dad hated to have my mother sort his things, he never changed the way he organized. Once a year when he was away, there was a thorough cleanup. The new house with the pretty yard that was part of their dream never became a reality, but my father found other ways to support mother's part of the dream. He set money aside to stucco and repaint the house; and, with delight, she chose the colors. It was not a surprise to my father when everything inside and out had a hint of pink about it. On Saturday, except in emergencies, Dad freed my sister and me from work in the fields to mow and water the yard. With some research, he discovered that pine trees like brackish soil. Several Christmases in a row we decorated potted Christmas trees and, in the spring, planted them in the yard, where they thrived and now tower around the old farmhouse.

A shared dream is like a handful of sand. Held loosely, respecting the hopes of both people, the sand remains where it is. But the minute you close your hand and squeeze tightly to hang onto your view of it, the sand trickles through your fingers. You may hold on to

Money Wrapped in a Dream

some of it, but most of the dream will be spilled and lost. Each partner must hold to his or her view of the dream with care. My parents learned how to dream together. "It will look better in the morning," they would say to each other; and it did, sometimes because she gave and sometimes because he did.

Money Wrapped in a Dream

Author's Note & Discussion Questions

Being partners means sharing the work and supporting the workers. The personal sacrifice required to sustain a shared dream brings the power to it. This give-and-take continues throughout the dream. Even as you embrace the same dream, you continue to value parts of it differently. Nowhere is this more apparent than in decisions regarding the allocation of financial resources. Reflect upon the story:

1. Did Ben and Ruth have one dream, two separate dreams, or two versions of the same dream?

2. What parts of their individual dreams did they sacrifice for a shared dream?

3. Did they ever resolve their differences, or were accommodations made?

Chapter Five
The Neighborhood

A community is the mental and spiritual condition of knowing that the place is shared, and that the people who share the place define and limit the possibilities of each other's lives.

-Wendell Berry

The large room vibrated with the buzz of voices, mostly male, blended young and old and punctuated by good-humored guffaws. It was evening, and though the gathering had been scheduled to begin several minutes ago, the men in charge were enjoying not being pressured by the clock. Boys, slicked up and pressed into scout uniforms, were still filing into the room, while their families found places on the metal chairs circled on the gymnasium floor. Seated on the stand, facing the audience, Ben watched as the boys entered. They were ill at ease in their uniforms and shuffled to the side of the hall, where they stood in bunches with their backs to the chairs, trying not to be recognized. Owning a scout uniform was a luxury for most of these families. Uniforms were handed down from father to son, to son, to son, loaned between relatives and only worn on special occasions. It was obvious by the bulging and straining of some of the uniforms that this had better be the last wearing, while for others it was difficult to find the boy in the fabric; cinched in at the waist and with pant legs and sleeves rolled up several times, these clothes were a lifetime investment.

Normally Ben would have been working with the other scout leaders, lining up the badges, sorting out the flag ceremony, and greeting boys and families, but tonight he sat in his uniform on the stand, where his knees wouldn't be bumped, watching. He had postponed knee surgery for years. The injuries had begun with high school football and gotten worse through the war years, but this spring, when the cow he was doctoring had fallen and pinned him under half a ton of bovine muscle, he knew something had to be done.

Postponing surgery through the summer and fall, he'd hobbled around until he could bring in the harvest. Just a week ago he had gone under the knife. Though the surgeon recommended operating on each knee separately, Ben, anxious to conserve costs and recuperation time, had encouraged him to operate on both knees at once. The days since the surgery had been pure agony. Ruth, aggravated by his unwillingness to spend time in the hospital to get the pain under control, had been nursing him at home, but even her best care had not saved him from nights of rolling around on the bed moaning and crying out in pain.

Finally realizing that neither of them was getting any sleep, he had moved his sick bed to a cot in the back room of the house where his cries wouldn't frighten the children. Tonight was his debut into public with crutches. The other leaders had assured him they could handle things, that he should stay home and rest, get well and take it easy. Even though she knew he had a good excuse to lie around, Ruth had encouraged Ben to come; it would make him feel better to be out among neighbors and friends.

From his vantage point on the stand, he watched the audience gather. Some were as familiar as his own kin, while others were still allusive to him. Ben was surprised at the emotion he felt. His life had rubbed up against theirs. They had shaped him. A tall, substantial man with sandy hair acknowledged Ben with a small jerk of his head and then took a chair toward the back of the hall. So Seth was here. Ben had met him nearly twenty years ago across the barrel of a shotgun. It hadn't been pointed directly at him, but nonetheless Seth held it in his hand in such a manner that Ben knew it easily could be.

"There ain't never been any fences here, and we ain't about letting them start now," Seth declared. He had not come alone; his father stood silent and foreboding at his side.

These were Ben's neighbors. Not much of a welcome. Ben straightened from the posthole he had been digging and turned to face the men, resting lightly on the handle of his shovel, his only defense.

"I'm going to fence my land," Ben replied, firmly drawing out the words so the two men understood. "This isn't community property. I'm planting wheat here. Your cattle trample these fields on the way to the river every day. You'll have to train them to get water another way. "

"You don't own the river," Seth growled menacingly, moving a step closer. "You don't have any right to block our path to it."

"It's going to take me a couple days to finish the fence. You're welcome to use that time to show your cows other possibilities, but they can't come through my land," Ben said decisively.

"Who do you think you are?" Seth blazed. "Just 'cuz you and your daddy have some high-and-mighty schoolin', you ain't going to throw your weight around."

"You're not welcome here," the old man spat, splattering the toe of Ben's work boot with tobacco juice.

"Sorry to hear that," Ben replied, struggling not to panic. Where was this going?

"There's ways we do things here, and no piece of paper changes that," Seth muttered angrily. "You can't fence us out. Our cows have just as much right to drink that water as yours do."

"They do," Ben agreed, "but not if they have to go across my land to get it." The air was charged, brittle between them. Ben stood like stone, hoping to stare them down, hardly daring to breathe for fear his movement would be construed offensively.

The sound of a car roaring onto the dirt road toward them broke the tension. Seth glanced in the direction of the noise and then stalked off across the field, but not before swinging the gun threateningly in Ben's direction, letting him know that things were far from settled; his father followed with a baleful look behind him at Ben.

Ruth was shaking with fear when she reached him. "What was that all about? What did they say to you? I saw the gun from the kitchen window, and it scared me to pieces. I didn't even take time to grab the baby. "

Her stricken face thawed him; Ben pulled her close, "It was their warning shot across the bow. They don't like the fence, and that was their way of telling me so. Thanks for coming to check things out."

"What if something happens to you? What if I'm not watching the next time they find you alone?" Ruth began to cry softly. "I can't stand at the window all day long, Ben."

"Well I'm glad you were standing there today," Ben conceded.

"I don't understand. It's our land. It's not as if we're doing something wrong," Ruth was wailing now. "All the effort we made with being friendly—the cookies, and trying to visit them. Not one of them would let us in or even talk to us."

"They're afraid, Ruth," Ben soothed, "afraid of change and what it will mean for their families."

"How could they possibly be afraid of us?" Ruth countered, stamping her foot. "We have nothing. We paid every penny we had for this place. We paid more than it's worth; I know we did. They're probably laughing their heads off at us."

"They don't know how to farm," Ben said, soothing her. "They've only ever taken from the land. They don't know how to plant it and mold it into something different from what it is now. They don't share our dream. The fence will keep their cattle from wandering through our fields to the river, but I don't think that's their real objection to it; there are water holes and springs all over the place where cattle can drink. I think the real reason they object to the fence is that it will keep *them* out as well."

"What do you mean? All they'd have to do is come to the door; I'd let them in. I'd welcome some company," Ruth affirmed.

"It's the men, Ruth. Almost every night they're traipsing along the river, setting their traps, hunting and fishing. With the fence up, it will be trespassing for them to harvest our pheasants."

Ruth considered for a moment then said, "Ben, these drains you're putting in should take the groundwater off their land as well. Why can't they be glad we're here?"

Ben didn't answer her question, his thoughts elsewhere. He didn't own the river, but his property ran right down to the bank on both sides, for nearly two miles along the marshy meadows. Though the farm had a previous owner, it had not been fenced or cultivated except for a garden patch and a cornfield near the house. Partitioning these fields had resulted in feuding in neighboring communities. "Father warned me that something like this might happen," he finally offered.

"Then why put the fence up now? Why not ease into it, a little section now and maybe more in the spring?" Ruth asked.

"Because it's easier now; there are no squatters living on our fields. People don't think they have to own this land to live on it. Any day someone could pull an old trailer in here and set up house, and we'd have the painful experience of trying to oust them."

"Then why not fence a path to the river that allows the neighbors to move back and forth without ruining our fields?"

"No, Ruth, they know we've bought this place. They're waiting to see what we're going to do with it. A path to the river would just confirm their thinking that they have some kind of rights here. The earlier we put this thing to rest, the better it will be for all of us." Ben was firm.

Through the fall, he'd finished fencing the perimeter of the farm, three rows of barbed wire on freshly cut juniper posts. But they were wary. Ruth made certain she was around if one of his brothers wasn't helping. Later in the year, when the ice piled up in the river and the resulting flood claimed almost half their farm, friends and family came from all over the county with teams and equipment to help dig them out, but none of the neighbors came. They drove by looking straight ahead, as if not seeing Ben made him cease to exist. At community gatherings, they were acknowledged only by outsiders, and despite Ruth's continued efforts to be a good neighbor, she had never been invited into their social circle.

While there had been no more open confrontations, there were small things that made Ben wonder if the game had gone underground. Late one evening, when he and Ruth returned home, they saw flashing lights in one of the outbuildings; the loud, rough voices and the sound of smashing glass terrified Ruth.

"Ben, who's in there? What are they doing?" She agonized as he turned off the car lights and eased it down the driveway, trying not to make sounds that would tip off the looters.

"I don't know, but I've suspected someone's been rifling through our things. This is the first time I've had any evidence," Ben responded, not taking his eyes off the lights flickering in the old building.

"What are they smashing?" Ruth questioned as the sound of breaking glass and laughter grew louder.

"Your fruit jars, and from the sounds of things, they're drunk."

"Oh Ben, take me away from here; let's take the children to your parents' house; then you come back with your brothers."

"No. I'm afraid they'll leave while we're gone and I'll never know who's in there or, worse yet, they'll start the place on fire. I need to confront them now. I want to know who's involved in this, " Ben said, reaching for the handle of the car door and pushing it carefully open.

"What if they're armed? Shall I go to the house and get your gun?"

"No, I don't want my gun; that would make things worse. It's probably just some local boys out for a night's fun, but, just in case, put the kids to bed, lock the doors and stay in the house. My pitchfork is right over there; I'll take that with me."

Ben carefully picked his way through the darkness and stood for several minutes at the door of the shed, watching. Three neighbor boys with lanterns were at work jerking the glass bottles from the boxes and smashing them, with a great deal of pleasure, against the other objects in the shed. As far as he could tell, they were not armed. He had seen all the boys before; the youngest was Seth's son, Fred, barely 12 years old. When the boys noticed him, they tried to rush the door, figuring he could only stop one of them. But the hand-to-hand combat training he'd received in the military came in handy. The next minutes were tense, but when the boys realized that Ben could take them, and he was serious about turning them into the police, they finally submitted to his terms.

It was a long night. Ben watched from a hay bale while the boys cleaned up the glass and restored some order to the shed, using the pitchfork several times when he saw they needed a little encouragement. When they finished, Ruth stirred up some pancakes and scrambled eggs and invited them in. At first the boys were sullen and unwilling to eat, but in the end their hunger and her cooking won out. Soon the boys were stuffing themselves. Before they left, Ben reminded them that they had agreed to pay for the broken jars by helping him with evening chores for two weeks.

The two older boys never showed, but the next evening, and every subsequent evening for the next two weeks, Fred came as agreed. Wary at first, he kept his distance, came and went with only a few grunts of acknowledgement. But one evening, despite his timidity, he couldn't hide his excitement; cutting across the field, he'd spotted what he thought was a blue heron and its mate. "Come and see," Fred invited as he ran back toward the field. "See if I'm right!"

Ben was not much of a bird watcher but followed Fred into the field to have a look. That had been the beginning. It was obvious Fred loved the wetlands birds that wintered along the river. As they watched the herons feed, Fred shared the names of some of the other birds and conversed easily about their nesting habits and the way they cared for their young.

"Fred, have you ever considered joining Scouts?" Ben questioned. "I'm working with some other boys studying animals and how they live. You have a gift for this kind of thing."

Fred never responded. They finished watching the heron and walked back to the barn in silence to begin chores.

A few days later, Fred had reopened the conversation. "I can't come to scouts. My dad's not home. I don't have a ride."

"Ride with me," Ben said casually, trying not to frighten him off, but again silence took over.

A couple days later, Fred reported that he would come a few times to see if he liked it.

As the court of honor now finally began, Ben's knees were already aching. He was beginning to wish he'd stayed home.

Fred had not only liked scouts, he'd loved it. He joined the troop, became a leader, and worked his way through the ranks with the other boys. Tonight he would receive the coveted Eagle rank. Ruth had reminded Ben of that while he deliberated about coming. It was easy to spot Fred towering above the younger boys. For the first time, he was wearing a uniform that matched top-and-bottom. Ben couldn't miss a night like tonight. In a year, Fred planned to graduate from high school. He would be the first in his family to attend a university. Scouting had nourished Ben and Fred's friendship. But it was an accident that opened Ben's heart to Fred's father, Seth.

The day of the accident had been cold and wet. A series of local hot springs regularly left a cloud of sulfurous vapor hanging over the river bottom, but on cold, wet mornings it mixed with the water vapor in the air to form a dense fog that obscured the valley floor. Unable to see the road clearly, a neighbor, with his wife and two children, had run head-on into a fast-moving milk truck. With a gash on his head, the driver of the truck found his way to Seth's house and reported that the neighbors were injured and trapped in their car. The news spread by telephone from neighbor to neighbor to neighbor; somehow, Ben and Ruth had been remembered and called.

By the time Ben arrived at the scene, most of the neighbors had already gathered. The road was blocked by the tangle of the sedan and the truck, and people were working to free the family. He fell in with them, helping where he could, smashing windows, soothing the frightened, sobbing children, and helping ease them through the narrow openings, past the shards of glass, into the safety of the school bus they were using as an ambulance. Leaving her children to care for each other, Ruth joined the women. They brought old sheets for bandages, quilts, pillows, and hot drinks from home and worked quickly to fashion makeshift beds on the floor of the bus, where the seats had been removed, and bandage and comfort the injured children. Ben watched as Seth grabbed the door on the driver's side of the automobile and, with brute force, inch by inch, bent an opening large enough to remove the father from the front seat.

The mother remained trapped deep in the car, her moaning barely audible. The truck had hit the front of the car on the passenger side, pinning her beneath the twisted metal of the frame and under layers of broken glass. Seth and the other neighbors worked at the metal with sledges, and then with bare hands, trying to bend it and free the woman, but it was no use; the steel would not give.

Finally Ben spoke up. "I'll get my torch. I think I can cut it." The others stared at him, some skeptical and disbelieving, others hopeful. They had never seen a metal torch, nor did they know he had one and could use it.

"Trying to be the big man?" Seth accused. Ben didn't answer, glad to do something that might help. He took one of the neighbors and headed home. It would require two men to lift the steel-wheeled cart with the heavy cylinders of acetylene and oxygen into the bed of his truck.

While he was gone, the men continued to work, but nothing changed except that the mother grew weaker, barely able to respond. They were running out of time. Handing his heavy welding apron to one of the men, Ben directed, "Put a bunch of heavy quilts on her; then put this on top of it to keep the sparks from burning her. The apron won't cover her completely, so get a couple buckets of snow in case the sparks get into the quilts. Some of you grab those boards and build some protection to keep the sparks from flying into the engine. I need help moving these tanks."

Suddenly everyone was busy. Seth muscled the steel-wheeled cart into position and stretched out the hoses. In a matter of minutes they were ready. "Whatever you do, don't watch the torch," Ben warned, putting on his welding hat and pulling down the visor. "It will burn your eyes, maybe even blind you. I'll tell you when I've cut through the metal and need your help. Your job is to keep the sparks from causing problems."

He had never used his torch to cut an automobile apart, let alone save a human life, and it made him nervous to have Seth standing directly behind him. This was much different than shop class had been. With all of them watching, he stood for several minutes a little confused, trying to determine where to make the first cut. Finally Seth touched the frame with his finger, indicating the place to start. His arrogance was galling. What did he know? Who was he to make suggestions? Ben bristled inwardly. Finally though, realizing he had nothing better to offer, he calmed himself and accepted Seth's lead. The rest was relatively easy. Seth indicated where each cut should be made, and Ben did the cutting. They rescued the mother far more quickly than Ben had imagined possible. There was genius in Seth.

The pain in Ben's knees escalated now, making him nauseous. Why had it seemed like such a good idea to sit on the stand? Why had he ever agreed to it? He was hemmed in on both sides, with his crutches under his chair so they didn't block the aisle. If he tried to leave, he'd have to fish for them and disturb the whole row trying to get out. He wished he was seated next to Ruth and she could take him home. She was smiling at him from the audience, encouraging him with her eyes. The awards were being presented; surely he could make it to the end. He just had to hold on.

After they had cut the mother free, Ben and Ruth helped the others quickly, but carefully, situate blankets under her and around the little family for warmth and padding. They called encouragement as the school bus pulled out and started down the road toward the hospital in town. "Hold on, hold on. You'll make it. You're going to be okay." When they lost sight of the bus, emptiness settled over those who had stayed behind, and the old-timers gathered in clumps to discuss what was ahead. Feeling on the outside of that group, Ben had helped Ruth gather their things. They were preparing to leave when Seth opened the circle and motioned them in.

"How will they ever pay for this?" breathed one of the neighbors.

"It will ruin them," anguished another.

"They're just getting started; this could lose them the farm," sorrowed another.

"Do they have any kin close by?" queried someone.

"No one close enough to help," replied a neighbor," I think their nearest folks lives hours away."

"I know about hospitals," Ruth ventured, feeling shy speaking in this setting. "I'm a nurse. They might be able to pay for a day or two in the hospital for a couple of them, but they can't afford to have the whole family cared for in the hospital."

"That man couldn't care for a newborn puppy for weeks," Seth concluded.

"What about his chores?" Ben asked. "Did he get to them this morning before the accident, or are they still waiting to be done?"

"Looks like we're the ones to help," another added.

The neighbors divvied out their care and their chores. Later that day, Ben brought home the sobbing little neighbor girl he had carefully eased through the broken window earlier that morning. The blood from the accident had not yet been washed from her face, and she was inconsolable. Both of her legs were broken and casted to the waist with a bar between her feet. She could only scoot herself around the floor. A few days later, when her mother was strong enough to be released into Ruth's care, her hospital bed was set up in their small living room, where she convalesced for a month. Ruth was the nurse, the laundress, and the dietician.

All around, neighbors worked to help. Ben watched Seth's lantern come and go early in the morning and late at night from the neighbors' barn. He milked their two cows and hauled the milk can to the road so it could be picked up and delivered to the factory, keeping the milk check coming. Another neighbor fed the stock with hay brought from his own stack. The father was soon able to return home and care for his little boy, but dinner was brought in to help them along. The service happened quietly. Ben was surprised that the neighbors never met again to check up on how things were going; they simply went to work. No money was ever exchanged; their service was freely and gladly given, a true gift.

Ben expected that things would change, that the neighbors would be friendlier, and that there would be more visiting back and forth in the neighborhood. But not much really changed; it just wasn't their way. Seth still passed Ben on the road looking straight ahead, as if they were strangers, the only difference being a small jerk of his head, an acknowledgement.

The pain in his knees was excruciating now, and it seemed a very long time since Ben had heard anything that was happening in the meeting around him. His eyes were closed, and he was focused on fighting back the nausea, trying to stay in his seat and keep things together. He was sweating; big drops of water were rolling down his forehead into his eyes. Suddenly he didn't care anymore; he had to get out of here and find Ruth. Ben tried to stand, but the pain buckled his knees, and he pitched forward into the row ahead. He heard the crash but no more. Everything went blessedly black.

When he drifted into consciousness again he was being carried and could hear Ruth's voice soothing him, encouraging him back. Who was carrying him? Ben couldn't open his eyes; the pain and nausea were still all around him. He heard the car door open and felt relief; they were going home. Strong arms eased him carefully onto the backseat and tucked his coat around him for warmth.

"Trying to be the big man?" a man's voice asked.

Ben managed a faint smile; he knew who it was, and it was okay. The question had come from a friend.

***

Even with all the help that was given, the accident did cost our neighbors their farm. The husband was never strong enough to farm again, and his wife continued to need assistance to manage at home. They left our community and moved closer to family, but when they left, though tears were shed, there was a great gladness that we had not looked the other way in their time of need. We stood taller as a family and as a neighborhood. The goodness we had discovered amongst ourselves elevated us, and we were richer because of what had been revealed about those with whom we lived. The lens through which we perceived each other framed a better dream than we had fashioned alone.

We do not dream in isolation from our family or our neighbors. Our dream rubs up against theirs and is threatened by humanness and imperfections. The lens through which we see our neighbors frames a best dream—one that takes them in—or one that is less powerful.

Money Wrapped in a Dream

Author's Note & Discussion Questions

    We are individual people, but the commonality between neighbors is greater than are the differences.

1. Ben and Seth had different dreams. What were they?

2. Why were their dreams a source of conflict?

3. Differences often take the form of diverse talents. If we're willing to accept differences in neighbors, we open ourselves to become recipients of their unique capacities. Why do these often come in the form of a surprise?

4. In what ways does sharing talents between neighbors create wealth in the community that transcends, but does not diminish, the benefits of pure exchange?

Chapter Six
The Hired Man

All successful economic societies are united by trust.

-Francis Fukuyama

There was smoke in the morning air—barely noticeable, but mixed lightly with the fragrance of new-mown hay, the barnyard, and the shimmering heat of the August sun. Ben felt the fire before he smelled it. The air was thicker, and the birds lining the low-hanging electrical lines were quiet, watching and waiting with none of their usual rumpus. Rarely disturbed by bonfires or occasional bouts of weed burning, they were an excellent warning system for the grass fires that seemed to begin spontaneously and sweep through the hills into the ripening fields of grain, creating a raging inferno.

The mood outside had drawn Ben from the house sooner than he had planned. Ruth's protestation that five days to recover from double pneumonia was not enough was accurate; but worries nagged him out of bed. Dressed in work clothes, he stood in the yard, looking around the valley at the hills, carefully scanning them for the irregularities that signaled fire. His jeans felt strange, stiff, and heavier than usual. Ruth had washed them and hung them on the clothesline to dry, just as she always did, but today it felt like he had belted on lead weights that winded him with every step. Standing in the yard, Ben finished snapping his cuffs. He loved these shirts. Purchased from the local implement store, they were just the right weight, like a second skin. Ruth had bought several with short sleeves, but summer or winter he preferred long sleeves that could be rolled up or down to accommodate the weather or the job at hand. These shirts had a bonus feature: two chest pockets with a flap he could fasten securely. His day book fit neatly into one, and his wallet slid perfectly into the other; spending 10 to 12 hours a day driving equipment made him loathe sitting on his wallet.

Ruth followed Ben from the house with a basket of wet clothes ready to hang on the line to dry. She stood still, watching him struggle to dress, noting the beads of perspiration that popped on his forehead with the smallest exertion. His dark wavy hair was cut shorter than she liked, in what he fondly called his summer 'do.' "What is it, Ben?" she asked. "Why can't you rest? What's bothering you?"

"I can smell smoke; there's a fire. All the grain is ripe and ready to cut; a spark would race through the fields and take it all. I need to check things out."

"Can you tell where it's at?" she inquired, crossing the yard and standing next to him. "Is the fire close?"

"I don't think so, but then you never can tell down here in the river bottom. I'll drive up and look around; things may look entirely different from the upper fields. I think the fire is across the river at the top of the ridge by the airport; that looks like a cloud, but I think it's smoke starting to gather above those trees."

"Well that's the *one* advantage of living by the river; it does make a nice fire barrier," Ruth added wryly. "I'll try and remember that the next time it floods. Surely this means you can go back to bed?"

"No, I can't rest. In an hour Jack should stop the combine for breakfast. I want to see how he's coming, how the cutting's going—"

Ruth stopped him, her hand firmly on his arm. "Ben, you can't be around grain dust—you're not well."

"I've got my mask in the truck. I just plan to look around," he assured her.

Turning to face him squarely, she made her appeal. "We were both foolish to think you could run the combine with a mask. You're highly allergic, and it's dangerous. Look at you, it's pneumonia in both lungs this year. Every year it gets worse."

"I'll be careful; I'm not planning to stay long."

"Ben, you heard what the Doctor said, any exposure could cause a reaction that would cut your breathing off completely. You could be gone before help came. I don't want *us* to end now," Ruth finished quietly, the tears shimmering but her no-nonsense eyes were direct and piercing.

He pulled her into his arms, laundry and all, and held her for several minutes, counting himself lucky for the millionth time. How many men had a wife like this? She was pure loveliness and a worker. It was just a little past seven, but breakfast was made, she was hanging out her second load of wash, and she was wearing lipstick. She always started the day with lipstick. It was her talisman, her signal to the world that she was ready for whatever came her way.

"Something just doesn't add up," Ben mused into her hair.

"What doesn't add up? "

"The numbers keep coming up short," Ben replied, avoiding her eyes as she shifted to look at him.

"Short? What numbers? In what way are they short?" she questioned, pulling away.

"When we shipped the sheep this spring, Jack and I counted and double-counted; we were 50 short," Ben started. "There were 50 fewer sheep in the field in March, when we shipped, than in October, when we bought them for fattening. That's a lot of sheep to lose over a winter. We always lose a few to coyotes and dogs, but never anywhere near 50, especially when someone is hired to watch them. That's the reason we kept Jack on through the winter; I figured with increased sheep profits, we could pay his wages, but we lost more sheep this year than any year previous. Funny thing, I took the horse and rode the fields trying to figure out what had happened; if the dogs or coyotes had gotten them I would have found their carcasses half-eaten around the fields, but I didn't find any sheep, dead or alive. It was as if the sheep had just vanished."

"That's why you were pouring over the records yesterday."

"Yes, but that's not the only thing."

"What else is bothering you?" she asked, almost afraid to hear the answer.

"Well, for the last few months the gas log has never been right."

"How could that be?" Ruth stiffened, suddenly defensive. "I know it's not the kids, Ben, and I know it's not me. I made an extra log for the kitchen. You've seen it, and we review it almost every night. Did you remember to add the two together?"

"Yes, but it still doesn't add up. At first I thought it was an error on the part of the deliveryman, but they've double-checked their records; they're not to blame for the discrepancy. In the past, our record of the fuel we've used, compared to what was delivered, has only differed by a few gallons. Since March, the amount we've used and that we've reported have been off by over 100 gallons."

Ruth stared at him. "Ben, how can that be? Jack is the only other person with a key, and I think he's been careful to write down what he uses. He's on the log. Do you think someone else has a key to the fuel tank?

"I don't know, "Ben said, turning away and walking toward the truck, "but I need to ask some questions."

Ruth walked to the clothesline and began hanging out the wash. Watching her work, Ben knew she was thinking over every possibility for the discrepancies except the one that was staring him in the face. It was too early to share his suspicions with her, but the incident yesterday had brought it to a head. While she was in town, Ruth had picked up the receipts from the Grain Growers showing how much wheat had been delivered for storage since his illness. Before pneumonia, when he had been running the combine, they had been hauling over ten ton of grain from the field every day. He knew it would take Jack some time to get the hang of the combine, but since his illness, less than two ton a day had been delivered from his fields to storage in town. What was going on? He had to find out.

The smell of smoke was unmistakable, and the fire, now visible in the clump of trees on the ridge, was gathering attention from the neighbors. Ben started the truck and watched the activity for a few minutes while he checked the gauges on the dashboard, undecided about what to do first. His fields were not the only ones at risk. Should he help with the fire or go to the field and check on Jack? With a wave to Ruth, he headed toward the gravel road that ran in front of their place. He would never forget the fire that had swept through his father's farm. Even after all these years, the smell of fire still set alarm bells ringing in his head. Ben turned in the direction of the fire.

The year of the fire, he had been six years old. The threshers had come the day before to harvest wheat and barley on his father's farm. It had been exciting, as a little boy, for him to watch them arrive, teams of horses and strange men filling the yard and the fields with noise. Ben and his younger brother had watched from the porch as the men worked through the day to fill the granaries with grain and then build a giant straw stack, with the stalks left from the threshing, next to the five large hay stacks his father had harvested, hauled and stacked during the summer—a year's supply of food and bedding for the livestock. His mother and sisters had bustled about since dawn to prepare the noon meal for the men, a massive spread crowned with a large tub of fried chicken. Underfoot in the field and in the kitchen, the boys had been banished to the porch, where they were ordered to stay until the men were gone from the fields.

Next morning the yard was littered with loose straw from the threshing, a pure paradise for boys. Captivated, Ben and his younger brother and their friends began to gather the straw and build smaller stacks next to the one giant straw stack they had watched the men build only yesterday. Ben couldn't remember whose idea it had been to find the matches and start one of their small stacks on fire; his mother had warned him repeatedly about playing with matches. When it was over, the horror of what happened made him too ashamed to own to the idea. The loose straw had gathered the fire from the small stack right toward the big one. His father, on his way home from the beet dump, spotted the smoke and began yelling at the top of his lungs, "Fire! Fire! Fire!" Hearing the yelling, his mother ran from the house and began gathering buckets and organizing them to haul water to the stacks. One of the big stacks was already on fire when his father stopped the lathered team in the yard and jumped onto the stack next to the burning one, shouting for water. They hauled bucket after bucket to him and watched as he poured the water over the hay, hoping to wet it down and halt the inferno, but it was no use; the fire jumped from one stack to another until all six were in flames.

Fear had been everywhere for Ben; fear of the flames leaping about the yard, burning everything they licked; fear for his father, enveloped in the blaze on the top of the stack; but worst of all, a sickening, dreading, blaming fear deep inside. He had helped initiate this.

The fire spread from the stacks to the chicken coop, the barn and the outbuildings. The animals cried in terror as smoke and flames filled the barnyard. His mother prayed. Neighbors came and helped rescue the frightened animals from the torched buildings and hung wet quilts over the back of the house to keep the sparks from starting it on fire. In the end, every bit of hay and straw burned; the chicken coop and barn, outbuildings, harnesses, and equipment were gone. Worst of all, his father's face and hands were severely burned. Most of the animals, the house and the garage, had been saved.

Wrapped in white bandages, his father had received the kindness and condolences of his neighbors. When the last of them had gone home, he gathered his family in a large circle in the living room and, despite the pain of the burns, knelt with his children and offered a prayer of gratitude that their lives and their home had been spared. Ben had sobbed openly during the prayer. Filled with remorse and guilt, he'd crawled into his father's lap and confessed all. He had been disobedient and broken a family rule, and his rash act had resulted in circumstances that had stripped their family of material necessities and had almost taken his father's life. They cried together, wetting each other with their tears. Finally his father looked him squarely in the eye and asked a question he had never forgotten: "Can I trust you?" Instantly sobered, Ben had realized he was being offered another chance, another opportunity to prove his faithfulness, to show that he could put the well being of his family above foolish fun. He wanted to be trusted. Grimy and tear-stained, he had nodded in the affirmative. That moment had shaped him.

Ben pulled the truck over to the side of the road and stepped out; the old agony was in his stomach. Was it leftover guilt, associated with the fire from the past, or something current, like the premonition, related to the missing sheep and the missing gas and the missing wheat? Walking through the weedy barrow pit and up over the rise, he could see the blaze spreading in a solid wall along the brow of the hill. Emergency equipment, cars and trucks were clearly visible, parked everywhere along the ridge. The river snaking through the valley provided an impenetrable barrier that separated his grain fields from the danger, but Ben wanted to join his neighbors and help out. On his walk back to the truck, he stumbled and fell over a partially concealed rock that hooked the toe of his boot. There was nothing nimble about his legs; lying in the dirt, he realized that, despite good intentions, he didn't have the strength to help anyone today. Dusting himself off, he determined to check on Jack and then return to bed. Hopefully, his neighbors would understand.

Not everyone had been as forgiving as his parents and the close circle of friends and neighbors that rallied to support their family after the fire. His mother lamented to her last days that she had been busy and had not given proper supervision. Yet months later, when the distant relatives saw the burns that remained on his father's face and hands and heard about the devastation to the farm, they wanted to know who was responsible for this awful thing. To them, Ben became the disobedient boy, the horrible boy, the thoughtless boy whose rash actions had started the fire that had stripped sustenance away from his family and had almost taken his father's life. Despite his parent's protestation, when those relatives gathered he heard small groups rehearsing to newcomers the story of the fire and his role in it. Perhaps that's why he had a soft spot for other people who'd experienced hard things in life or were down on their luck. He couldn't pass them by without reaching out, hoping to make life a little easier for them. Ben had known many men without a dream and in need of a meal, a friendly smile, and a helping hand.

Jack was one of these. He and his wife and two young sons had started as neighbors but had been bumped from pillar to post, forced to move their few possessions from almost every shanty in the community because of Jack's alcohol addiction. They had next to nothing; everything of value had been sold to buy liquor. His children were shy, thin, awkward and belligerent, hanging out with the tough guys in school, struggling to learn and doing little that would prepare them for life. His wife, Marie, was small, blonde and afraid. Jack was a decent guy, friendly and a big talker, full of promises that in the end he could never keep. Ben had encouraged Marie to find a treatment facility and check him in. "If he'll get help, I'll hire him. You can live in the home on the upper place," Ben promised. Marie had taken him at his word, appearing at his door almost two years ago to collect on the promise.

When Marie's knock came Ben had been surprised, but pleased, to see them. "Come in," he had invited, looking them over quickly as they moved inside. Marie was wearing the tan trench coat she had worn since they'd first met, wrapped taut and held in place against her thin frame with a man's leather belt, and her purse was clenched tightly to keep it closed. Jack was thin, nervous and unsure; his eyes darted up and down, looking everywhere but at Ben. Finally, he took a chair and stared at the floor.

Seated, Marie came right to the point. "We've come to take you up on your offer. Jack here has been released from the hospital. We're ready for work and that house you promised." There it was, laid out unmistakably between them.

"Are you ready to work, Jack?" Ben inquired quietly, trying to feel him out.

Jack hesitated before answering, still not meeting his eyes. "I'm a bit weak, but I can do what you need me to do."

Now it was Ben's turn to stare at the floor, unable to speak for several minutes. The silence between them became anxious. He had offered in good faith, and they had taken him at his word. He wouldn't go back on his promise, but he needed to help them understand the responsibility that came with the offer. Outsiders had no idea of the sacrifice that building this place required. Far from having extra cash lying around, he and Ruth were still developing the infrastructure. All the money they brought in went to make improvements and meet payments. He and Ruth lived with careful frugality, willing to surrender luxuries for the dream of a home, space of their own and enough work and opportunity to prepare their children for lives with a future. Jack wasn't applying for just an ordinary eight-to-five; crop tending didn't keep a clock, and far from glamorous, it was filled with dirt, drudgery and every kind of inconvenience. Did Jack have the doggedness to follow through on the menial work that would be required of him? Could Ben trust sharing their dream with him?

Ben gathered himself. "Jack, I need you to look me in the eye."

It took awhile, but finally Jack's eyes met his and stopped their furtive casting about. "Jack I'm not as concerned about your ability to work as I am about your willingness to do the work you're asked to do," Ben said. "You'll get the hang of the farm work—"

"I sure do want this job," Jack interrupted, bringing a smile to Marie's worried face. "I'll do whatever you ask; you can depend on it."

"You can't drink while you're working for me," Ben said, speaking directly, "not a drop of anything with alcohol, and that includes wine and beer. If I even suspect that you're drinking, you'll be off the place the same day. I don't believe in second chances. If you're not willing to make that kind of agreement, you should leave now."

"I'm not drinking no more," Jack quavered.

"Can I trust you?" Ben asked, not moving his eyes from Jack's face, quietly waiting for an answer.

After some minutes, Jack looked him in the eye and with assurance said, "You can trust me; you'll never need to worry."

"You can't work for me if I can't trust you. If I ever doubt that you're holding up your end of the bargain, you'll be gone," Ben promised.

"Don't worry about that, mate," Jack pledged, some of his old bravado returning. "You won't regret this decision."

Ben hadn't regretted it. Jack had a ready wit and was teachable; it felt good to see the old house lived in by a family. Marie pulled the weeds in the yard, planted some flowers and hung curtains in the windows. They started to smile more, and Marie began going places without both fists clutching her purse. It had taken time for Jack to clear their bills and save a little cash to begin building a dream of their own. This spring they purchased chickens, 50 little balls of fluff that Marie got cheap at the feed store. Jack found some lumber lying around and built an enclosure next to the house, where they could keep an eye on them. He strung up a heat lamp to keep them warm and patrolled the yard a couple times each night to ward off predators. It pleased Ben to see their family huddled around the chickens. When the chicks got big, the family planned to kill one or two of them each week so they had a proper Sunday dinner; the others were going to be laying hens so Marie had eggs for cooking. No, he hadn't regretted it—until a few months ago when things had started not to add up.

Ben reminded himself to slow down as he pulled into the driveway. The chickens were mature now. They had outgrown their enclosure and wandered freely through the yard and grain fields, surrounding the house foraging for food. He scanned the wheat field, searching for the combine, and was surprised to spot it parked near the truck in the far corner of the field. It was just a little past eight. He had expected to see Jack in the house eating breakfast, but his timing must be off. He had missed him. This was a 100-acre field, and walking to the combine would do him in, but there was nothing else for it. He had to see Jack today.

Resolutely, Ben started on foot across the stubble; he couldn't risk a spark from the engine of his truck starting a straw fire. Despite his fatigue, it was emotionally exhilarating to walk this field. Planted in wheat for the first time this year, it boasted an amazing crop, stalks rising six feet tall with heads over four inches long. He smiled at the memory of his young sons trying to move the hand lines to water the field; the only thing visible had been the swaying of the wheat and the head of the riser moving almost robotically through the field. Surveying the field, the old panic seized him; the field was over half cut. What had happened to the grain?

He was wheezing. Ben slowed his pace. Walking with his head down, he began to notice wheat spilled on the ground in regular intervals. First, just trickles, as if Jack had not emptied the bin of the combine when it was full. That was understandable; a newcomer might do that a time or two before he got the hang of things and emptied it earlier. Surely Jack would notice and adjust. But he hadn't noticed; the spilling increased and continued across the field. Alarmed, Ben suddenly realized what must have happened. Jack had emptied the wheat from the bin of the combine into the truck and forgotten to turn off the auger. With the auger on and the combine running, as soon as grain was fed into the bin the auger picked it up, sent it up the spout, and spit it immediately onto the ground. This was worse than anything he had imagined. Why hadn't Jack noticed? Surely he must have heard the sound of the auger. Why hadn't he wondered why the bin was never full? Tons of wheat were scattered in the dirt all across this field, and there was no way to retrieve it. Despite fatigue, Ben marshaled his reserves and quickened his pace toward the combine in the corner of the field.

Drawing close, he realized there was no movement around the combine or the truck. What a strange place to park, here at the far end of the field, away from everyone and everything. Where had Jack gone? Surely not back to the house. No one was around the place when Ben had pulled into the driveway, and he hadn't passed anyone on the way to the field. The combine was parked too far from the truck for the spout to empty the grain into the bed, but Jack had emptied it anyway. Sick at heart, Ben inspected the pile of grain lying on the ground beneath the spout; the squeaking of the auger moving up and down in the empty bin told the story.

"Jack… Jack…Jack!" Ben bellowed repeatedly, his angry voice echoing through the field, "Where are you?"

Slowly, the door of the truck inched open, just enough to allow Jack to slip to the ground. He was wrinkled, bleary, red-eyed and unsteady. He hastened to close the door of the truck behind him, but his attempt was too slow to halt the cascade of liquor bottles that followed him onto the ground.

"I was just taking a nap. You know it gets tiring running that thing," Jack said thickly, pointing to the combine, trying to bluff his way. "What a bore, around and around you go. Glad you're back to take over gov'nor," he said, finishing with a little bow.

"Pack your things, Jack, you're finished here. Get off the place. I want you out of here today," Ben ordered.

Jack began to cry, blubbering out apologies. "I just slipped a little. It's only happened once. You'll see, I can stop. This doesn't make any difference. It won't happen again. You can still trust me."

Pieces about the missing sheep and the gas began to come together in Ben's mind, and he spoke the thoughts as they formed. "You stole the sheep and sold them for booze, didn't you? It was a long winter; you didn't think I'd notice," Ben said, trying to be matter-of-fact as he walked to the truck, took Jack's things from the cab and piled them on the ground before he locked the cab and pocketed the keys.

"I can pay that back to you," Jack protested. "It's the only thing I've ever taken. Take it out of my wages."

Walking to the combine, Ben climbed up onto the deck, turned off the auger and locked the gears so it couldn't be moved; then he placed the key in his pocket.

"What about the fuel you've been taking, Jack? Didn't dare drink in town—too many people there know about our agreement. You've been using that gas to drive all over the valley to find booze and company to drink with," Ben said, not really wanting to hear Jack's defense; he'd begun coughing and knew he had to get out of the field.

"You don't know that's me. Could be just one of your brats not writin' down the numbers and then blamin' it on me so they don't have to take the heat," Jack flung back thickly.

Ben was coughing hard now, spasm after spasm raking him, twisting and tearing at his lungs. He stumbled to the tire of the combine and curled himself into it, lying there for several minutes, fighting for breath, trying to get control. Finally, he gathered the strength to stand and begin the long walk from the field. Stumbling, Ben looked down at his feet; he was standing in the pile of wheat Jack had unwittingly unloaded onto the ground.

"How did this wheat get here?" Ben demanded.

Jack stared at the wheat littering the ground. A look of surprise crossed his face, as if he was seeing it for the first time. "Please give me one more chance. You'll see; I can do it. Give me one more chance," Jack pleaded.

"No," Ben said, numb with the pain of it, "I can't trust you. Get your things; I'll walk you back to the house."

Anguish filled him, and the old agony churned in his stomach as he started out across the field; smoke from the fire dulled the air, robbing the cheer from the morning brightness.

How would he make his payments? This loss was worse than anything he had imagined yesterday when he reviewed the numbers. The wheat that lay scattered all over the field had been slated to pay off the debt on the combine. Where would he find the extra to make it up? Not only was the profit from the crop gone, but he had lost experienced help and would be short-handed the rest of the season. He couldn't run the combine. Who would finish harvesting the grain?

The sound of a man's gulping sobs brought Ben back to the moment. At first he thought the cries were his own, the agony within him swelling out into the air; but then he realized they were coming from someone else. Someone behind him was weeping. Remembering Jack for the first time since he'd started for the house, Ben stopped and looked back. Still under the influence of the liquor he'd consumed, Jack was weeping copiously and struggling to stay erect. In his arms he carried his jacket, gloves, lunchbox and other personal items that Ben had taken from the cab of the truck. On a normal day they would have been easy to manage, but as he stumbled across the field, weeping out his grief, they slipped constantly from his grasp. Seeing the broken man, Ben realized he wasn't the only loser. For Jack and Marie and the boys, their dream was gone; the old cycle had begun again. Ben waited and allowed Jack to catch up with him; reaching out, he took the lunchbox and jacket from his arms. They crossed the rest of the field together.

***

It was Christmastime, and the loud, late-night knocking at the front door roused the household. Soon we were jostling around my parents, trying to see who was out there and why presents were piled high and deep on the front steps. Jack, with Marie, wrapped in the tan trench coat, stood at the bottom of our steps.

"I've come to pay you back, "Jack said, indicating the heap of presents. "I've made some mistakes, but I'm going to make it right. I bought something for everyone."

A chorus of excitement greeted his announcement, and we surged forward to claim the gifts, but my father blocked our way.

"That's kind of you, Jack," Dad said, "but we can't accept them. You need the money to take care of your own family. Take these gifts back, buy some food and give your kids a Christmas. We're fine; we have all that we need."

We were stunned at my father's words. What did he mean we had all that we needed? I could see the gifts on the steps. Some of them were not wrapped. There was an electric frying pan, a new toaster, and a pink electric blanket, my mother's favorite color. We had none of those things in our home, and with the loss of the wheat crop, we all knew there wouldn't be anything like that under our Christmas tree. We were devastated.

My father walked out onto the porch and closed the door behind him, leaving us inside to glimpse what happened next through the picture window. Standing together on the walk, he and Mother, Jack and Marie talked for what seemed a long time. We pressed our faces against the window, fogging it, then held our breaths, clinging to the hope that Dad would soften and let them bring the gifts inside. In the end, they cried together, and Dad helped them carry the gifts back to their car.

In a few years, Jack and his family returned to our small community. Jack never worked for my father again, but he began to work for other farmers in the area, and he rented a small house in which Marie hung curtains. Dad was a scout leader for one of his boys, and I noticed on several occasions that he sent him home with a big bag of potatoes and a roast from our freezer. My father fired Jack, but he did not reject him. Dreams require trust and the muscle of self-control.

Money Wrapped in a Dream

Author's Note & Discussion Questions

The fruit of a good dream doesn't just appear by happenstance; it is built on the bedrock of sound principles. Dreams that have the power to bless generations are shaped upon a foundation of integrity.

1. Why do we speak of virtues like honesty, dependability, cooperation and commitment as necessary foundation blocks upon which to build a dream?

2. Considering Jack, what are some reasons for the importance of these virtues?

3. In what ways does Jack impact the life of everyone in the story?

Chapter Seven
Saying Good-bye

Advice is like snow; the softer it falls, the longer it dwells upon, and the deeper it sinks into the soul.

-Samuel Taylor Coleridge

Nurses with brisk voices and orderlies with carts could be heard in the corridor going about their business, but the room in which Ben waited was quiet. The lights had been fully on and bright when he'd arrived, but he had adjusted them, leaving only the small light above the bed glowing and the shades open to encourage sunlight from a winter morning to soften the austerity of the room. Waking in a hospital would alarm his father, Ray, but the room felt better now, and he slept peacefully, giving Ben time to think.

Though in his mid eighties, Ray did not look like a sick man. There was very little gray in his thick, dark hair. He had creases but few wrinkles on his face, and his complexion was still ruddy from weather and sun. As Ben studied him, he realized there were fewer laugh lines. It had been years since Ben had seen Ray's face split ear to ear in amusement. Though he had aged gracefully and with only minor limitations, life in Ray's later years had taken more concentration. Never a tall man, in his prime Ray stood about five feet, five inches tall, with square shoulders, erect head, steady eyes, and the stocky bulk of someone who depended upon his muscles daily. Through the years his posture had remained erect, and his frame was trim now. Ben was several inches taller than his father and thirty-seven years his junior, but he had inherited the same muscular build and dark wavy hair.

The hospital room was cheerless. It helped Ben to think back and recall real days with his father; times he'd known couldn't last forever, but in the thick of living it had been easy to assume their perpetuity. The call from the hospital had come suddenly. "It's his heart," the doctor had said. "There's an arterial blockage." How surreal to be sitting here now, looking on while his father fought to live. Ben had rarely seen him in bed, let alone in a hospital gown. How small and vulnerable he looked. This was not at all like him, and that awareness made Ben extremely anxious.

Movement from the bed caught his attention, and Ben smiled as Ray opened his eyes carefully and tried to comprehend his surroundings without lifting his head from the security of his pillow.

"Not exactly where I expected to see you today," Ben began.

His father acknowledged him with a faint smile. "Came on suddenly… thought I'd eaten the wrong thing for supper."

"Mother called to let us know what had happened. Ruth and the kids send their love."

Again Ray nodded, but only his head moved; the rest of his body seemed clay-like, anchored to the moorings of the bed.

"I just came from a meeting with the banker and planned to drop by and see you at home anyway," Ben said conversationally. "I've got the money for the loan payment I owe you and mother in my pocket."

"How'd it go?" Ray croaked out.

"Fine; after I made the payment, they signed the paper saying that my account was paid in full."

"Good," Ray murmured.

"After last year and that episode with the balloon clause, I don't think I'll ever take the experience casually again though. Without your help, I wouldn't have a farm this year."

Talking was taking a toll on Ray, so they sat together quietly, remembering the events of just a year ago. The mortgage on the 1,000-acre dry-farm had been amortized on a 30-year payment schedule, but the document contained a balloon clause that effectively required the balance to be paid in full at the end of the seventh year. Because this had not been disclosed at the time of closing, both Ben and Ruth were unaware of the clause until last fall, when Ben met to settle his accounts at the bank. Scraping together the yearly mortgage payment had taken all his resources; there was no possible way to pay the mortgage in its entirety as required by the balloon. The balloon clause was a shock to Ben, but the worst part was realizing he'd been set up. The banker had purposely waited seven years, long enough for him to bring up the water from his original acreage, put the 1,000 acres under sprinkler irrigation and tie the water legally to the larger property. The contract had been written in a way that would force foreclosure and give the bank ownership of the entire farm. The water was worth far more than the land, and though the banker feigned regret, Ben sensed his underlying glee. He would have lost the entire farm if his father had not loaned him the money to cover the payment.

"You know the banker, don't you father?" Ben asked.

"Yes, he comes from an old family," Ray whispered. "They've been in the valley longer than your mother and I."

"But you've never done business with him?" Ben posed, hoping he wasn't pressing too much.

"Never needed to," Ray said slowly between breaths. "My father got me started here…I made my payments to his bank and never bothered to change things after I paid for the farm… always seemed nice not to have the neighbors know all my business."

Ben waited, allowing his father to rest, and then added, "After I bought the 1,000 acres, the banker drove out my way a lot. At first, I thought he was coming to see how we were doing, to encourage me, but he never stopped to talk. Even at the time, it seemed strange to see him creeping along, looking things over, and I wondered why he was so furtive. You know no one accidentally comes our way, especially in a fancy black Oldsmobile. A couple times I saw him with some cronies, stopped alongside the road and looking over my fields, but they always drove off before I could speak to them."

"He was a good man," Ray said, rubbing his chest, obviously in pain now, "just got mixed up in things he shouldn't."

Alarmed, Ben stepped to his bedside and touched the call button.

"Ben," Ray continued, struggling to talk between gasps, "Learn from this; don't get involved coveting another man's dream."

A moment later, a nurse appeared, and Ben was ushered into the waiting room while the doctor attended his father. Not into reading popular magazines, he found a chair in the corner of the room, away from the traffic surrounding the magazine racks, and unsnapped the flap on the pocket of his shirt, took out his daybook and rummaged for the short pencil he kept alongside it. This tiny book contained his calendar, yearly farm record and other important entries. Ben turned to the back of the book and found the section reserved to record early-morning thoughts and advice he didn't want to forget. It was easily the thickest section because, yearly, he cut these pages from the old daybook and pasted them into the new one for safekeeping. Over the years, much of the counsel he had copied into this book had come from his father. Last year, after the bank debacle, he had written, "Find a banker you can trust," and, "Don't let your neighbors know all your business." Carefully, Ben found a blank page, dated it and wrote, "Don't get involved coveting another man's dream."

Glancing around the waiting room, Ben noted there was still no nurse with news of his father. Returning to the daybook, he turned the pages slowly, reading one entry and then the next. They were memorable and stirred a flood of memories that transported his mind from the apprehension of the moment to the drama of another. He would never forget the first year they'd farmed the big farm; it had been eight years ago, 1961.

The wind had whipped across the field, cold and filled with sand that cut like shards of glass. Ben turned his back to the fury and pulled up the collar of his jacket to protect the tender places on his neck. It was the first day of May but felt like the first of March; all around him swirled an eddy of gritty wind blowing mercilessly at the tiny plants, severing their newly formed leaves and covering the shivering stalks with a spattering of dirt.

"Father, let's go," Ben had called to the silhouette of his father in the distance.

Money Wrapped in a Dream

Lifting his head, Ray had looked in Ben's direction but kept walking slowly through the wind across the top of the field, stooping every now and then to dig in the soil with his fingers, seemingly oblivious to the weather.

Remembering that his father was recovering from a cold and that he had promised his mother they wouldn't be gone long, Ben called again, repeatedly, trying to get his attention. "Let's go, Dad, time to leave."

When Ray responded to his call, Ben motioned with both arms, beckoning toward the truck. By now his father had walked much of the 70-acre field, starting at this end, going to the top, crossing and crisscrossing the furrows, stopping all along the way to inspect the soil and the condition of the young plants. His father was thorough; that was his way. Ben kept waving and calling until he saw Ray turn and start back across the field. Having gotten his father's attention, Ben made his way slowly back to the truck. He was haggard and hollow, exhausted to the core. How well he knew the size of this field. Kicking his boots against the tire to remove the dirt, he opened the door and climbed into the cab to wait.

It seemed like forever since Ben had slept more than a few minutes, and most of that rest he'd gotten lying here on the front seat of the truck. For the last three days and nights, with the help of his oldest son, Mark, he'd been moving sprinklers on three-hour shifts, hoping to settle the sand and keep the small plants from being blown from the field. Three-hour shifts were a killer. It took

15 minutes to go each way between the house and the field and another hour to move the lines. With only an hour and a half between changes, they hadn't bothered to undress and put on pajamas before climbing into bed. Mark had even stopped washing up. Ruth plied them with soup and hot drinks while they pulled off their boots and wet clothes. At first it had been fun, a real adventure, father and son going together into the dark of the night to slay the dragons, so to speak; but as the alarm continued to relentlessly jar them from slumber, Mark became so tired that Ben had ceased to wake him. Without Mark's help, it took longer to change the lines. Taking a thermos and a sleeping bag to the field, Ben had slept in the truck for what seemed just minutes between changes. Exhausted from lack of sleep and discouraged by what appeared to be a losing battle, Ben dozed while he waited for his father and tried to forget that outside the shelter of the truck a coarse, rough wind was cutting the life from the small plants as effectively as a guillotine.

The sound of the door creaking open startled him awake. Ben waited while his father got settled on the seat beside him before asking, "Well, what do you think?"

"Don't know," Ray said, pulling the cab door closed against the wind.

"Think I should disc it up?" Ben asked. "The leaves are gone, and what's left of the plants is covered with a half inch of dust."

"I think you did the right thing," Ray said slowly.

"What right thing?" Ben asked.

Money Wrapped in a Dream

"Putting the water on it," Ray answered. "If those plants have any chance at all it's because the soil underneath that dust is wet."

Ben sat staring straight ahead through the gritty windshield. "When I bought the place, the banker said this land wasn't fit for row crops. He recommended raising hay and grain and milking a herd of dairy cows."

"Why didn't you follow his advice?"

Ben didn't answer right off. This was his first crop in this field. When the banker had agreed to finance the 1,000-acre purchase, he made a lot of recommendations about the place, more than Ben had felt was needful. Settling back into his ornate leather arm chair, the banker had shaken his finger at Ben and said, "Laddy, you put in a dairy with 100 head of milk cows and raise hay and grain on those new fields. That's the way you'll make it. Cows require constant attention, but they bring in steady income. Twice a day you're putting money in your pockets and mine. Row crops are risky in this country."

"I'm not a cow man," Ben reminded his father. "I wouldn't like 100 cows all that much, and besides, I don't have the knees for milking twice a day."

Ray nodded, thinking it over.

"Father, look out there, look at that field; there's never been a 70-acre patch of sugar beets raised in this county. It looks like the fields upstate from us, open countryside under sprinkler irrigation. They're starting to have phenomenal success. I think we can do the same here." Enthusiasm edged into Ben's tired voice. "Look at those rows, so long you can barely see the end of them.

Think of it, just an up-and-back with the harvester and you've done an acre—no more endless turning around in narrow fields."

"You forgot the part about the soil," Ray reminded him.

Ben's smile was his first in days. His father meant it to be a joke. They'd discussed this so many times they knew each other's lines.

"The soil is light and sandy, perfect for sugar beets and potatoes. Probably too light," Ben admitted, laughing now at the sand caked by the wind across the windshield. He put the truck in gear and started for home.

His father grinned back. Ray had been a truly successful farmer. It had been their quiet talks together that had encouraged Ben's decision to purchase the dry farm. Out of habit, Sunday evening, Ben's car found its way to his parent's home, and while his mother entertained the children with stories, he and his father talked about life and land. The original river-bottom farm had been a disappointment; despite tremendous expense to drain and level the fields, the production still wasn't sufficient to support his family. Thoughtful, well-read, and a man of experience, his father was a remarkable sounding board for Ben's plans and questions. Familiar with homesteading and taking land from sagebrush to productivity, he had walked these fields more than once with Ben, helping him shape the dream.

"Before this wind came up, it was sure pretty to see the plants mark the rows clear to the end of the field," Ray observed.

Money Wrapped in a Dream

"I'm afraid that's history," Ben said. "If I don't hurry and plant it again, I won't even get a crop off this piece. I'm afraid I'd better disc it up and put it into wheat."

"How will you make your payment if you put this in wheat?" Ray asked. "I thought this field of sugar beets was your cash crop."

"It was," Ben answered. "I've got to plant something that pays in this field. It's too late in the season to replant the beets; they'd never mature by fall. It would be tight, but I think we could make the payment with a good wheat crop. We'd have to sell most of the hay, hope we got a good price for it and put the two profits together."

Ray was quiet, looking into the dashboard. "How's your operating budget? How much of it have you spent on this field?"

"A lot—most of it," Ben confessed. "I didn't have all that much to start with; the banker wouldn't advance money against what he called a 'phantom crop.' I have the same as I had last year—oh a little extra, but nothing like we really need for this place."

"Wait a day or two," Ray recommended, opening the door and getting ready to leave. "Let's look at it again when the sun is out. I best get home before your mother worries."

Ben felt comforted, the gladness of a man that knew true mentoring. He watched his father walk to the car, remove his boots and put them in the trunk so they didn't soil the floor mats. He knew his father, solid and silent over trouble, would go home and pray.

A few days later the wind stopped blowing, and his father drove into the yard as Ben was putting diesel in the tractor. "Been up to the beet field?" he asked.

"No, there hasn't been time," Ben admitted. "Did get some sleep though, so maybe now I can face it."

"Get in," Ray said, "let's take a look." Ben got into the car and rode with his father to the field.

"Have you been up there?" Ben inquired as they rode.

"Every day," Ray confessed.

When the car climbed the last hill and the field fell into view before them Ben couldn't believe it. The sugar beets had pushed up through the dust and leafed out again. He could see small plants marking the full length of the rows all across the field. "Well I'll be darned!" Ben exclaimed. "Did you know about his?"

"I saw it yesterday, but I didn't want to ruin the surprise," Ray chuckled. "Thought this might happen; the other day when I was in the field digging around the plants I had a notion new leaves were forming."

Springing from the car, Ben whooped and yelled, threw his hat into the air and then jumped around, trying to catch it. His father watched, deeply pleased.

"They won't take much thinning," Ray commented as Ben climbed exultantly back into the car. "Pretty sparse in parts."

Stopping at the house, Ben twirled Ruth around the kitchen and shared the news. There wasn't time or money for a real celebration, but their dream had survived, and the lilt was back in their steps.

Money Wrapped in a Dream

There had never been much money to throw around, but that summer and fall stretched the definition of basic living. The bank was not the only establishment in town unwilling to advance a line of credit beyond previous limits. The seed, fertilizer, and equipment companies capped Ben's line of credit at his prior level; anything needed beyond that had to be paid in cash, and cash was dear. Taking on the additional acreage changed things at home. In the past they had milked about 20 cows to supply the family with milk and Ruth with income to manage the household, but Ben no longer had time to manage the milking. Everyone was needed in the field. His sons, who were capable of milking, were needed to set the lines and move the sprinkler pipe from station to station bringing life-giving water. Ben turned the milking over to his daughters, but, unaccustomed to working with livestock, they were afraid of the big animals and, at a time when they needed maximum cash from the dairy, milk production dwindled to almost nothing. Ruth resumed full-time work at the hospital to help buy basics, but most of her income went to pay farm bills.

By the fall of the year the entire family was tired and stretched thin. Every loose penny and extra ounce of energy had been gathered up and put to use. Back to school had been tough. Usually a celebration, with a shopping trip to buy new clothes and shoes, pencils and notebooks, was planned, but this time there simply wasn't money for any of that. Old shoes were looked at carefully, passed down and repaired at the shoemaker shop. Ruth washed and starched old clothes, let down hems and patched jeans. It was hard to see the children leave for school feeling like last year's leftovers. On top of that, the community was at work to raise money for an addition to the local hospital, and Ruth was asked to help raise funds. She organized the bazaar, collected items to sell, found an auctioneer and made food for the bake sale. The night of the fundraiser, they couldn't even find a quarter to send with her to purchase a sandwich. Discouraged, Ruth had wept in Ben's arms. The next morning, Ben took her to the 70-acre field, to look at the sugar beets that were thriving in the sandy loam.

A hand on his shoulder stirred Ben from his reverie. It was the nurse from his father's room, reporting that he was resting and stable. "Try not to excite him," she cautioned.

Slipping quietly back into the room, Ben sat once more on the chair by the window. Ray was peaceful, breathing deeply and easily, his hands and face the only parts visible outside the neatly turned bedclothes. Nurses came and went, checking and recording numbers; easily, casually, routinely, like this was just another patient. Watching them drove Ben crazy. Why didn't they take it more seriously? This was a big deal. Did they have any idea what was at stake here? In the hospital bed, Ray looked like just an ordinary man—feet, legs, arms and hands—nothing that let the staff know the stature of the person lying under that quilt, the work he'd done or the lives he'd shaped. Ben wanted to stand outside the door and instruct them,

"Hey, this isn't just your run-of-the-mill patient; this is my father. Look sharp." Taking out his book, Ben comforted himself in the pages of another time.

The harvest season of 1961 had been filled with high spirits; great relief that the crop was finally mature mixed with anxiety that the weather would turn foul or in the end the yield would not be enough to meet payments. The beet harvest was a communal affair. Before his father retired from farming, he had purchased a beet harvester and topper, which Ben and his brothers shared. They all contributed tractors, trucks and drivers to the crew, and they worked in a rotation until the harvest was complete. Each had years when their fields were harvested first and years when theirs were last. This year Ben was last. This was not his first experience with being last, and he knew the perils stormy weather would bring: boggy fields and frozen beets that could not be lifted from the ground.

Ruth felt the anxiety most; she was home, working away from the harvest, worrying and waiting, watching the sky. Like Ben, she knew they had to have this crop to survive. Through the summer, Ray had been a frequent visitor, dropping by with garden produce or apples from his orchard, checking on them. In the fall, he became the messenger bringing updates about progress in the fields.

It was late afternoon when his car pulled into the drive. Ruth rushed to meet him, anxious to save him the walk to the house and get the news. Forgoing the usual pleasantries, she blurted, "Did they finish? Will they be here tomorrow?"

Ray smiled at her impatience. "Yes, they were finishing as I left. They'll need to lubricate the equipment but by noon tomorrow they should start here."

"Thanks, Father," Ruth said, squeezing his hand through the open window of the car. Through the years he had become just that to her, a father. "Thanks for bringing me word."

"Ben said to have the boys clear the sprinkler pipe from the field tonight; he's kept the field wet to keep weight on the beets, but he needs it moved by morning."

"They're just home from school. I'll tell them," Ruth assured.

As quietly as he had come, Ray backed down the driveway, out onto the road and, with a wave of his hand, headed home. Ruth stood for a moment, appreciating his kindness.

Next day the harvest had begun. Down and up, down and up the long rows Ben drove the harvester. Ruth watched as the trucks streamed past the house on the way to the sugar factory loaded with beets from their field. Ray picked up the strays that shifted from the loaded trucks as they crossed the swale or fell to the ground while changing trucks under the spout of the harvester. He stacked them in neat piles and admonished the incoming drivers, "Pick up these beets and throw them into your truck." It took almost three weeks to finish the field. Even when the sky clouded up and poured rain they could work after just a few hours because of the light sandy soil. Ben's beets were the last patch harvested in the county.

On the day they finished the sugar beet harvest, the initial excitement associated with bringing in the crop was long past. Out of necessity every extra man and boy had returned to school or other pressing work, leaving Ben and Ray to dig the last few rows from the field alone. Reluctantly, Ray abandoned his job of collecting strays and drove the truck. Knowing that his father preferred a horse and was nervous about keeping the truck properly aligned, Ben slowed the pace of the harvester. As they finished the last rows, Ben jumped from the harvester and met his father as he climbed from the truck. They thumped each other soundly on the back in a celebratory embrace.

"Come with me," Ben invited. "Let's take this last load to the factory together and check on the tonnage." Ray nodded, climbing back into the cab of the truck, this time on the passenger side.

Conversation with his father had been easy on the way to the sugar factory that day; they were bringing in the last load and talking openly about the miracles that had attended the season, beginning with the remarkable new growth after the sandstorm had ripped the leaves from the beets and covered them in dirt.

Now, seated by Ray's bed, Ben read the words he had recorded that day years ago. "You know, son," his father had said as they pulled into the plant, "you got a miracle this year, but you can't always count on that. You've got to figure a steady way to make this place pay. You can't finance a dream on luck."

Conscious of tears running down his face, Ben wiped them with the backs of his hands, closed the book and secured it again in his pocket. The corridor outside the hospital room was suddenly noisy with voices and carts, drawing Ben from his thoughts. His father was deeply asleep and had remained peaceful for several hours. Ben felt hopeful. The hospital staff was changing shifts, and it was time to go; there were chores waiting. Others in the family would arrive soon to sit with his father through the evening. Gathering his coat, Ben bent and kissed his father good-bye.

Walking from the hospital toward his truck he felt the desire to drive along the old highway toward the sugar factory just as he and his father had done that day eight years ago. Instead of driving directly home as he had planned, he turned east, wishing it were possible to turn back the clock. In his mind, it was.

When they had reached the factory with the last load, the clerk had been surprised to see them. Usually growers gave the company at least a week to complete their tally and prepare a receipt before they stopped for the report; so Ben's request to wait in the office for the tally was an unusual request. He and Ray found some folding chairs and perused factory pamphlets and farm periodicals while the clerk worked. Her fingers flew on the adding

Money Wrapped in a Dream

machine as she tallied the numbers; finally, she gave Ben a record to take home and compare with his own.

Not wanting to appear too anxious, they had walked in silence back to the truck and waited until they were seated to examine the form. "The total tonnage was one thousand, three hundred eighty tons," Ben read from the receipt. Taking his daybook and the short pencil from his pocket, he worked the numbers. "Let's see, 70 acres of beets, that's 23 ton per acre. Incredible! I've never had a crop like that." Ben was jubilant. Thirteen ton was the breakeven point. He had prayed for 18—that was the tonnage they needed to pay the mortgage and the bills on the farm. They had extra!

"Check the math again," Ray cautioned. Ben ran the numbers as Ray rechecked the report.

"You're right, it's 23 ton to the acre. That's a mighty good yield," Ray acknowledged, the lines in his face relaxing into a broad smile. "I'm proud of you, son."

Parked in the circular drive in front of the factory, Ben now tried to remember the feelings of that day years ago. Thumbing the pages, he looked for the other entry. They had sat quietly for a few minutes, glad for each other, for the strength that came through their association and for the success of the season. Then his father had advised, "You have a lot of needs. It will be easy to let the farm gobble up all the profit. But Ruth and the kids have sacrificed as much as you have. You have a little extra; spend some on them, but spend it on something that gives back."

Slowly Ben closed the little book, snapping it back into his pocket. Chores were waiting, and Ruth would be anxious for news from the hospital. He started the truck and turned toward home.

It was 3 a.m. when the call from the hospital came telling them that Ray had slipped away quietly in his sleep. Ruth wept openly, but the shock spurred Ben out of bed, into his clothes and toward the hospital. He knew there was nothing he could do, but he had to do something. His father had died alone; Ben had not been there to see him off, to ease his way, to express his love. He wanted to see Ray again, to feel him and to hold his hand until there was no trace of earthly warmth remaining. He wanted to say good-bye before it was public and confusing.

The nurse at the night desk was one of Ruth's friends; she recognized him and stood to walk with him, but Ben discouraged her, mouthing, "I want to be alone." Nothing had changed about the room except that the shades were drawn. The dim light still glowing above the bed gave a sense of privacy and respect to the stillness of death. His father looked as if he were peacefully sleeping except that no breath stirred his limbs. Ben was glad he had come. Bending, he kissed Ray on the cheek and then carefully eased himself onto the bed, stretching out by his father's side and laying his arm across his chest in a final embrace. With his mouth next to his father's ear, Ben began to talk, to share the experiences remembered through the day, to thank him for the legacy he'd passed, for the dream Ben carried—the dream that had been shaped first in the heart of his father before it had sprung into his own. As he talked, tears of gratitude flowed, and the comfort Ray's presence still brought settled around him.

***

The year we had "extra," Dad surprised the family with an organ for Christmas. None of us expected it; after all, we already had a piano. It was surprising that Mother was so happy; unlike my father's mother, she was not a gifted musician. The present was not directly for her, but for her children, and somehow that mattered more. Our organ was not ordinary; while it could sound like a church organ, most of the time it didn't. It had a synthesizer, drum section and a preset rock n' roll beat that was in high demand. It delighted my mother to hear our happy voices and watch us boogie to the music. The organ brought merriment to the rigor of our lives. Dad had given a gift that gave back.

Later Dad changed bankers and put in a dairy with 100 head of cows that fed on the abundant hay and grain that grew readily in the fields. As foretold, it stabilized the farm. Dad never abandoned his dream of row crops, especially in the 70-acre field, and worked to improve the markets within the community to support them. We still had times when we prayed for miracles, but never quite like 1961.

Dreams are possible. My father brought to our family a dream he'd learned from his father and which my grandfather had learned from his. Not consciously conveyed, it was almost as if it sprang from the water or from the land these men loved. Sharing the dream amongst them multiplied its meaning. Having lived some aspects of my father's dream qualified my grandfather to be a mentor; however, his willingness to give advice and then look away and allow my father to pursue the dream as he uniquely saw it allowed both the dream and their relationship to flourish.

Money Wrapped in a Dream

Author's Note & Discussion Questions

All good dreams benefit from a mentor, "an interested other" or a father figure.

1. In what ways was Ray's mentoring helpful, and to whom?

2. Contrast Ray's mentoring with the banker's. How were they different?

3. What might be the difference between coveting and greed and just wanting more?

4. Of what value was Ben's daybook?

Chapter Eight
Building the Dream

*If you have built castles in the air, your work
need not be lost;
that is where they should be.
Now put the foundations under them.*

-Henry David Thoreau

Clouds of dust swarmed the pickup as 13-year-old Jim careened down the dirt track through the sand hills. Since it was a blistering August day, too hot to have the windows closed, he drove with them open, gathering speed to gain some distance on the billows of dirt and sand churned up by the wheels. The truck didn't have air conditioning, and the only relief from the heat came from the outside air blowing in. The gravel road was deeply rutted, and drivers like his sisters, who used their brakes on the hill to keep from going too fast, were a personal pet peeve; trying to stop on the hill dug the gravel out of the road in regular intervals, resulting in washboard ruts that rattled your teeth. Jim made it a practice never to sissy up and apply the brake. That said, he knew his dad would not be pleased to see the truck bouncing and skidding side-to-side through the ruts. Ben had repeatedly cautioned him against speeding. Having Jim drive at all was operating on the edge of the law.

It was legal for underage drivers to drive farm equipment to and from the fields as long as they didn't access main thoroughfares. Jim was small for his age, with dark, wavy hair, dark eyes and a permanent tan. He had been on the seat of a tractor pulling equipment along the gravel roads that connected the fields to the home place for years, but when he started to drive the truck the neighbors were alarmed. Because he was too short to be seen over the steering column, they were nervous to see an apparently unoccupied vehicle approaching them on the road. The sheriff pulled him over and cited him for dangerous driving; issuing a ticket that required both him and his dad to appear before the judge. In the end they paid a healthy fine but were able to work out a compromise that allowed Jim to operate the truck on farm roads if he were seated on a four-inch foam cushion that made his face visible through the windshield.

Jim knew he was driving too fast and it was dangerous, but he was teed off, and it felt good to punish the truck on the ruts. Frustration from the morning was still percolating inside him. He had been removing the sprinkler pipe from the wheat field when his dad stopped by.

"When you're done hauling the pipe out of the wheat, instead of storing it by the barn, set it up in the triangular field so it's ready to go," Ben called from the seat of the tractor. "Remember to double-line the sandy part so you can start them sequentially."

"We just finished watering that field," Jim protested. "It won't need water until next week, soonest."

"Lay the lines now. We won't turn them on until the field's dry; it will save time to have them ready."

"The field's too wet to get the pipe trailer in and out without mucking it up," Jim countered.

"Don't muck the field up! If it's too wet, park the trailer on the edge of the field and carry the pipe to the first valve." Without waiting for more discussion, Ben had driven off toward the hay field.

That had done it; the inferno started inside. It might save time, but it was coming at the expense of his back! All morning he had carried 20-foot sections of pipe from the trailer, parked at the edge of the field, through squelching mud to the valve. To top it off, there hadn't been enough useable pipes to double-line the lower half of the field. If someone didn't get them fixed he'd have to move the field in four-hour shifts. It chafed him. Despite the disagreeable nature of the work, he was glad for the physical exertion; it had taxed his muscles and numbed his mind, demanding every reserve. Fatigue lay like a welcome blanket over the strange inner turmoil that had eaten at him for weeks.

The one bright spot in the morning had been the cake. While he was eating breakfast, his mother had been preparing dessert for dinner. He had watched her slide a chocolate cake into the oven and then set about preparing nuts and coconut to be stirred into the frosting. German chocolate cake was his favorite. The image of that cake on her pedestal plate had gotten him through the drudgery of his morning work. Dinner was served at 1 p.m. sharp; if he hurried he might get a snitch of the frosting while it was still warm and gooey, before it had time to set. Thinking about the cake had distracted him from the jolting of the truck, but as he felt the back end coming around, trying to change places with the front, he knew things were getting serious. Edging forward on the cushion and moving the steering wheel instinctively to counteract the slew, he rode it out.

The pounding of the ruts popped open the glove compartment, and the contents burst from the confinement of the box and spewed out onto the floor of the truck: a hammer and wrench, nails, wire, wire cutters, screwdrivers, soldering rods, bolts, washers, gloves, receipts, crumpled tissue and the inevitable copy of the *Popular Science* magazine. Everything you needed to fix a minor emergency was kept in there, and now it was see-sawing about, rolling beneath his feet as he worked to control the truck, adding to his irritation. The only thing not rolling about was the magazine that had flopped open on its spine, the pages rifling open and shut in the breeze from the window. The magazine was for emergencies as well; sometimes the tedium of farmwork was unbearable.

The subscription was still in his big brother's name; but it had been years since Mark had come to work with them in the field, carrying a copy of the magazine stuck in the front of his jeans and hidden beneath his T-shirt, waiting for a quiet afternoon hour and a shady spot to sit down and read. None of them were as "died-in-the-wool crazy" about everything written in *Popular Science* as Mark had been, but they still carried a recent edition of the magazine in the truck. He had taught them how to endure the monotony of farm work, and following his example, the other children had rumpled and smudged the pages with frequent use.

Mark was the oldest in the family, and despite nearly a decade of years separating them, Jim had watched and learned from him. Two weeks ago, Mark had left for the east with his wife. Accepted at a prestigious graduate school, he had gone to pursue his dream. Mark was determined to grow wheat, but not on the farm; it was the sixties and, taken by possibilities beyond planet earth, he wanted to grow wheat in space and feed cosmonauts. His leaving had sucked the energy from the farm and dug a pit in Jim's stomach. Jim had watched while his dad and mother let him go.

Saying good-bye had seemed to take forever. In the weeks before he left, Mark had come whenever possible. He rode with his dad in the truck or perched himself on the back wheel cover of the tractor, talking over the putt of the engine. Jim felt more than a little annoyed and had justified it on several counts. First, there was a lot of farm work to be done, work that Mark had usually helped with but that he didn't pitch in to do now. He just sat around talking. Who did he think he was, some kind of hero? Why didn't he help anymore? Second, not only was Mark not helpful—he had been bossy, chiding them regularly about stepping up and doing more around the farm when they were already working their tails off. And third, Mark had spent a lot of time with their dad in private conversations. This exclusiveness really ate at Jim. It got his goat to see them deep in discussions that didn't include him. As a family, they had dreamed openly, out loud and together about the farm. Building the dream required all of them. They were all hard workers, and age had never before been a factor in having voice in a conversation. Working the dream required their collective effort. Why had his dad let Mark leave? How would they build the dream without him?

Mark was a budding genius with the welder. Even during his college years, he had come home on weekends to mend leaks in the miles of aluminum sprinkler pipe that carried water out over the farm and improvise equipment that made their work easier and more efficient—innovative equipment like "the wedge." Mark built it on the base of an old cultivator, using tractor seats collected from across the county. Pulled by a tractor, it allowed six people to sit with their feet on a plank and thin the sugar beets to a prescribed spacing while the row passed beneath them. It saved the pain of trudging up and down each row bent double over a short-handled hoe. With close to 100 acres of beets to manage, "the wedge" saved time and money. They couldn't hire anyone to do what Mark knew to do. Who would pick up the slack?

It wasn't just picking up the slack that bothered Jim. Who would teach him the ropes, the little things that made the long hours of farm work possible for him? He was a cripple, born with a club foot. The early years of wearing corrective casts day and night had kept his right foot from growing; it was a full two sizes smaller than the left, flat and red. Farm work required constant walking, chasing critters, doing chores, hauling hay, moving sprinklers, shoveling ditches, and his feet hurt constantly. Sometimes they hurt so badly he couldn't walk, so he'd take off his work boots and carry them, preferring to go barefoot rather than endure the pain of his shoes. Other times he'd wear them on the wrong feet, which, surprisingly, helped for a time.

Mark had looked for Jim in the fields and given him a ride whenever possible to spare his feet. He had taught him little things that brought comfort to the work—like how to keep warm and avoid freezing when driving a tractor at harvest time. There were no tractor cabs to offer protection from the danger of frostbite. Mark had shown him how to stand on top of the tractor and warm his frozen body parts over the stream of hot air issuing from the exhaust pipe. When his legs were numb, he'd lift his trouser legs and let a blast of the hot exhaust balloon up his pants. The continuous burst of hot air shooting up his clothes to his neck felt marvelous. He stank like diesel fuel, but the warmth coursing through the folds of his clothes was well worth it. The two brothers had worked side-by-side and relied on each other.

The dreaded day finally arrived, and the family had gathered to see them off. Mark and his wife were driving from the western United Stated to the eastern seaboard. Excited for the adventure, but without funds to rent a moving truck, they had taken the backseat from their small sedan and strapped it to the top of the car, extending the packing space through the trunk and up to the front seat. Nothing was in boxes, and none of their clothes were on hangers, allowing them to pack everything flat in the bed of the car, using their clothing to cushion things that were bulky or fragile. Front to back, the car was packed solid and level with the back window. When they could find no way to fit Mark's bicycle inside, Ben had helped him tie it to the grill on the front of the car.

"You look like something out of 'Grapes of Wrath,'" Ruth had quipped as she came across the lawn carrying a basket of food she had prepared. Handing the food to Mark, she gave him a squeeze. Though they had just risen from the table, it was her way; she knew that in a few hours they would be hungry and homesick.

"Thanks Mom," Mark said, handing the heavy basket to his wife.

Tired from the strain of packing, she had protested. "I don't know where to put this. We don't have room. Let's just get stuff along the way."

"You're kidding," Mark countered. "There's a whole chocolate cake and two quarts of peaches in there!"

"Even if I could find space for it, we can't possibly eat all this," his wife had said, not yielding.

"I'll find a place for the cake and the peaches even if I have to carry them all the way on my lap," Mark declared, climbing into the car to help find a spot.

Seeing the pain in Ruth's eyes, Ben stepped in. "You'll be glad for it. When you're traveling, there's nothing like a taste of home."

In the end, there had been a lot of hugging and kissing, waving and yelling good-byes, and then they had stood together, trying not to bawl while the car went down the road, across the bridge, and out of sight. Jim had watched his dad pull the handkerchief from his pocket, blow his nose loud and long and hurry off to the barn. Mark was gone; he had driven away from the dream.

Since Mark had left, except for the short-lived telephone call a week ago reporting their safe arrival, there had been no news from them, and nothing had really changed that much around the farm. They were still teetering in limbo, waiting. They couldn't go back to the way things were, but they didn't know how to go forward either. Something needed to propel them onward and into the unknown, and things had to change soon. The combine was already working in the field, harvesting the wheat, there was a stack of sprinkler pipe that needed mending in front of the barn, and all the third-crop hay was cut and raked, waiting to be baled, hauled and stacked. Each day at dinner Jim expected his dad to redraw their work assignments and present a plan of how they would proceed, but so far nothing had happened except that his parents spent a lot of time together talking. They'd better figure it out soon.

Dinner was a powerful magnet that drew them together, pulling them from responsibilities all across the farm. It was their chance to refuel and rest, to report in, catch up on what each other had been doing, and glimpse the world outside the farm. The mail came before noon each day and was placed at Jim's dad's plate, complete with bills, letters, the newspaper, and magazines. Ben opened the bills at the table but rarely discussed them unless there was some excess, like the light bill that he wanted to make a point about. He was neat and opened and refolded them just as they came, but Jim could tell by his grunts and grimaces how he felt about the contents. The arrival of Ben's favorite news magazine was a time of celebration, and he would sometimes read whole articles to the family, hoping for discussion. Even in years of poverty they subscribed to a newspaper. Though Jim was mostly interested in the comics, his dad talked about the headlines and the markets and then often napped with a section of the paper lying open on his chest. Letters from family members were kept to the last and read during dessert. His mother would hang over the back of his dad's chair, resting her arms on his shoulders while he read, trying to soak in everything the paper could tell her. It was not unusual for them to kneel in prayer for the sender after they read the letter. Dinnertime offered more than just food to keep them going.

Jim parked the truck next to the house and switched off the engine just as his brother, Will, walked into the yard, dressed in waders and carrying a shovel over his shoulder. Flood irrigating was a man's job but Will, 16, was cutting his teeth on the cornfields next to the house. Tractors hitched to the hay baler and pipe trailer stood motionless in the yard, announcing that his dad and brother were already inside, as were his sisters, who had been weeding sugar beets. He was late. Remembering the cake, Jim pushed opened the door and jumped to the ground, but his foot slipped on the wrench that had escaped from the glove compartment, and he pitched forward toward the dirt. Small for his age but agile like a cat, he recovered without the humiliation of a face-plant, but the torque twisted his bad foot painfully.

"Ouch! Oh! Damn!" Jim yelled as he hopped around in agony, irritated over the injustice of it all, "I'm dying, and they're inside eating cake!" The open door of the truck allowed him a view of the mess of tools littering the floor. His dad would be upset if he left this for someone else to clean up. Gritting his teeth, he got back into the truck, scraped everything into a pile and then stuffed it back into the glove compartment, pulling the cover down over the jumble and hoping it would close. But the lid to the box refused to latch. Unwilling to dump it out and start again, Jim applied some pressure on the lid with his knee, pushing slowly but firmly until he heard the latch click. Successful, he headed for the house.

Pushing open the kitchen door, Jim peered around, taking inventory, looking for the cake. His dad had his back to him and was talking on the phone, the long cord stretched as far as it would go in his attempt to find a quiet place. Jim's sisters were putting mashed potatoes, gravy, roast beef, and vegetables into substantial bowls while his mother washed pots and pans in a sink of sudsy water and his brothers scuffled in the hall. The cake was on the kitchen counter just behind his dad, but well within his mother's view if she looked in that direction. It was just as he had imagined: four lovely, chocolaty layers spread with thick honey-colored frosting that oozed down the sides of the cake. It would take a miracle, but Jim went for it. With his eyes fastened on his mother's head, he tiptoed backwards across the kitchen until he was standing in front of the cake. Just as he reached back to scoop up a puddle of frosting from the cake plate, her voice rang out, "Jim, get your fingers out of the cake!"

"Mom, how did you know I was here?" He demanded, indignant at the injustice of being caught just before the sweetness of success. "I watched you the whole time. You never saw me; you were scrubbing pans. Do you have eyes in the back of your head?"

"I saw you pull in and knew you'd head for the cake," Ruth smiled and then drawled in her deep voice, "I've been waiting for you."

"Come on, Mom," Jim wheedled, "I just need one little taste before dinner, just one."

Still on task, her hands working quickly in the soapy water. Ruth laughed and nodded her head in the direction of the mixer. "I left some frosting in the bottom of that bowl for you; it's been by the stove, so it's still warm, just like you like it."

Elated, Jim found a spoon and advanced on the icing but not before he draped a dusty hug around his mother.

Ruth didn't have a favorite son, but her relationship with Jim had always been special. Jim knew it was because of the hours she'd spent praying for a miracle, praying for his foot to heal, praying that he could walk, even run. Born in a small rural hospital, with a badly clubbed right foot, he had been discounted as a hopeless case by the doctor.

"He'll get along," he had announced as Ruth and Ben agonized over the small foot that rotated inward and lay almost flat against the inside of Jim's leg.

Thankfully, his parents had been unwilling to accept that pronouncement. Jim was old enough to appreciate the disfigurement he'd been spared. He had seen men with club feet as they "got along," shuffling down the sidewalk and nearly walking on their ankles. Somehow, his parents had managed to find money for the trips to the city, fees for specialists, surgery and the constant array of casts and special shoes that accompanied those visits. His right foot was far from perfect, but he could walk, and he could run.

Jim licked the last of the frosting from the bowl just as his dad hung up the phone and called them to dinner. Noting that Jim was still covered with mud, Ben motioned him to wash up before he sat down at the table. Jim's mother was a great cook, but she refused to serve anyone who hadn't washed up or who had his shirt off. "I'm not raising heathens," she'd announce, and they all knew they would starve if they didn't comply. Dinner was their board meeting after a busy morning in the fields, and they made their reports over steaming plates of food.

"We need to make some changes," Ben announced.

At last. Jim sighed inwardly and felt everyone at the table come to attention, interested to see how this would play out.

"I need to fix the pipe lying in front of the barn so we can keep the water going. I can't bale hay and do the welding. Will can't irrigate the corn and bale the hay. Jim, I need you to run the baler, and I need you to learn how this afternoon."

Jim was exultant. Out of all the things he could have been asked to do, he hadn't expected this. Baling hay was something men did, not 13-year-old boys. None of his friends knew how to operate the baler. Cows were fussy about their hay; it had to be prepared just right. Except for the baler and the combine, there wasn't a piece of equipment on the place that he couldn't handle, though he detested running the cultivator in the sugar beets; that was just plain boring. He was developing into the best equipment driver in the family, and it pleased him that his dad recognized his talent. Deep in congratulatory thought, he lost track of the conversation at the table until he heard his sister, Mary, burst out.

"Dad, I'm not going to drive the grain trucks up that big hill into town—it scares me."

"All you have to do is shift the axle, Mary, and the truck will make it without a hitch. I've shown you how; it shouldn't be a problem."

"I know you've shown me, but I still can't get the hang of double-clutching the axle. Sometimes it works for me, and sometimes it doesn't. What happens if I'm on the hill with a load of grain and the low axle won't engage? Please let me do something else," Mary pleaded.

"Mary, there's no one else to do it," Ben said. "I've thought this through carefully."

"Why can't Jim take the truck into town?"

"He doesn't have a license; you know that," Ben said, the color rising in his cheeks, "The sheriff looks the other way on farm roads, but he won't do that if Jim takes the truck into town. You're going to have to do it, Mary. Jim can ride with you the first few times, but after that you're on your own."

Ben pushed back his chair and rose from the table, signaling the end of the conversation and the end of dinner.

Later that afternoon, after work, Jim limped back to the house. He'd stayed in the field and run the baler as long as he could, even after his dad left, to gain confidence and work out some kinks before he had to operate it alone and in the dark. But, after a few rounds, he had to stop; the hay was just too dry. Coming to the house to get a few hours of sleep before his first all-night vigil, he noticed Mary climbing into the cab of the grain truck and knew she had waited for him. She was cutting it close. They would have to hurry to deliver the load before the grain elevator closed. Jim was anxious to get some sleep but headed for the truck instead.

He had been driving since third grade while Mary, four years his senior, had never voluntarily driven anything. The problem with Mary's driving was that she didn't do enough of it. She was only called on to drive in emergencies, and then the pressure of the situation usually resulted in disaster. He had rescued Mary from a few of those—like the time she ran the tractor into the back of the barn and the time she knocked over half the hay stack pulling up too close. Mary needed more hours behind the wheel when she wasn't expected to do something complicated. This was not one of those times; shifting the axle required skill.

"Thanks," Mary said, her face lighting visibly as Jim slipped in beside her.

"I've got to get some sleep, so let's get there and back as soon as possible," Jim said. "You drive, and I'll shift."

They had driven like this before and were comfortable with the task ahead. He sat on the floor and prepared to shift the lever on the axle while Mary started the truck, turned it around in the yard and drove down the lane and onto the highway. Because he was small for his age, no one could tell he was present; to any passerby it would look like Mary was driving solo. To get the truck into the compound gear, you had to shift the axle. It was the lowest gear and ideally suited to pull a heavy load up a steep, sustained climb.

His dad, Ben, was good at recognizing the different gifts of his children. They depended on Mary to organize the neighborhood kids that thinned and weeded the row crops and to keep them on task. Jim had total admiration for her. Weeding was hot, boring and never-ending, and except for the two weeks she took off to prepare for school, the crew was in the field almost every day. Jim and Mary were close, but he hated working on the crew. His attitude regarding weeding irritated her, and she was forever on him to slow down or, worse yet, to re-do his entire row. Thankfully, he was only assigned to the crew once or twice a year, and it was a relief to both of them when someone showed up in the field and took him away. He loved the independence of being behind the wheel of a vehicle and in charge.

"Jim," Mary spoke as she drove, "What would happen if I didn't shift the truck into compound? If

I started the truck up the hill and just used the other gears, could I make it to the top?"

"What! Are you crazy? You're thinking of skipping compound and starting up the hill with a loaded truck?" Jim was incredulous.

"I'm just asking," Mary said. "Don't jump all over me."

"Well, I think you'd probably get to the top of the hill, but it would be really hard on the engine," Jim responded.

"I'm just trying to figure out my options."

"You sound like someone who's about to be executed."

"That's about how I feel. You won't be with me, and I don't trust myself to shift the axle alone. I have to figure out another way," Mary reasoned.

"Dad will skin you alive if he finds out," Jim cautioned.

"You're right; but since I have to do the job, I'd better find a way that I can do it."

Jim was silent. It was dangerous to drive the big truck without using compound, especially when it was loaded. Skipping the gear early on, when the truck was just getting moving, or failing to shift into compound on a steep incline could damage the engine or the transmission, or both, resulting in expensive repairs. It wouldn't be pretty if Dad found out what she was doing. But in some ways, what Mary said made sense. Wasn't that what all of them did when they faced tasks that were too big for them? They found another way.

"Well, if you're going to try it, get your speed up first," Jim counseled. "Don't poke along like you usually do on the flat stretch before the hill; keep the truck moving. Once the truck starts slowing down, you'll have to shift down to get enough power to make it up the hill. Stretch every gear before you shift, get over to the side of the road, and don't be nervous about going slowly on the hill. When you hit first gear, you need to be almost to the top, because you won't have another gear."

Mary smiled for the first time since they'd started out. "Thanks for the advice."

They rode easily together the rest of the drive into town, but on the way home Jim asked the questions. "What did you think when Mark drove off like that?"

"What do you mean, what did I think? You didn't actually think he was going to turn down that offer and stay, did you?" Mary asked.

"Yes, I think he should have stayed."

"Why?"

"Because he owed it to the rest of us."

"Jim, Mark's doing just what he always dreamed of doing," Mary reminded.

"I know, but doesn't that seem kind of selfish to you, selling out and doing what he wants to do, not caring about Dad and the rest of us and all we've dreamed and planned?"

"What are you saying?" Mary asked.

"Well look at Dad. I mean, it's been pretty hard on him since Mark left—not just the extra work, but his leaving sucked the air out of the farm. Things have to change here."

"I know, Jim; that's why I'm driving this truck," Mary said emphatically.

"It's not just about you driving truck," Jim said with exasperation. "It's not just the extra chores. It's about what we're really trying to do."

"I don't get it."

"Think about the potato fields. You saw them when the only thing growing there was sagebrush and jackrabbits. Then we brought the water up. Now the potatoes in that patch are the best in the county. We could add 20 more acres to the field by filling in the gullies on the east side of the field. But how will we do that with Mark gone? It won't happen; it can't. We're all too busy just doing the basics—"

"I think Dad encouraged Mark to go," Mary cut in.

"Impossible. Dad's not half-done with what he's planned around here," Jim shot back. "We finally have all 1300 acres under irrigation. There's plenty of work and dream for all of us. Most of the main lines are buried, and there are wheel moves in some of the bigger fields. All it takes to start the water is to roll the lines to the main line, connect them and turn the valve. No more hauling pipe to and from every field every time we need to water. Dad set that up, organized it and paid for it. Who's going to do Dad's work now that Mark is gone?"

"I know it's a big disappointment."

"It's more than a big disappointment!" Jim railed. "I'm mad. From the time I was tiny I've worked and

Money Wrapped in a Dream

slaved with the rest of you so the bank didn't take the farm away. Now, just when we're getting ready to fly, Mark walks out!"

"The dream isn't over; Dad's doing Mark's part."

Usually comforted by conversations with Mary, Jim glared at her in disbelief. "Haven't you heard anything I've said?" He demanded. "This isn't just about getting the work done; this is about building what we've dreamed—that takes time and talent; with Mark gone, we're short on all of it."

Now Mary was yelling. "Jim, cool down! I don't understand why you're upset. Mom and Dad always planned we'd go away to college; we haven't taken an extra dime for all our work on the farm. Dad promised he'd pay our way through college; that's the way he's paying for my hours in the sun. I plan to take him up on it, don't you?"

"Of course I do."

"Then why are you so upset at Mark?"

"Because he's not coming back!" Jim bristled. "It makes me angry that so much of what we dreamed won't happen. It hurts Dad too."

"Do you plan to come back after college to run the farm? Is that what you want to do with your life?" Mary probed.

"I don't know," Jim admitted.

They were home now. Mary pulled the big truck into the yard, parked it next to the shed, turned off the engine and stored the keys in the holder on the dash. As Jim opened the door to leave, Mary asked, "Do you worry that with Mark gone you won't be able to leave?"

It was quiet between them. Outside it was already dusk, and he would only get a few hours of sleep before it was time to start baling, but the question remained. Is that what his turmoil was about? Was he afraid he wouldn't be able to leave and, in the end, would be left here working on someone else's dream? Jim turned and headed for the house.

After dark, the yard seemed unreal and ghostly. Baling hay had to be done at night. In the heat of the day, the baler pulverized the stems, and the sweetly flavored leaves were severed and lost. It was the sweetness of dried alfalfa leaves on the stem that enticed the cattle to stuff themselves. When there was a little dew, the stalks would bend and fold, with minimal damage to the leaves. Though the sky was clear and studded with stars, the only real brilliance shone from the large fixture on the pole by the barn, encircled by gnats swarming to the light.

Ben lubricated the baler and instructed Jim again in the basics of diagnosing poorly formed bales. Quick to catch on to mechanical things, his dad had a set way of doing things and was not always a patient teacher. He expected you to listen and follow instructions. Jim tried not to interrupt, get offended or make excuses—that part was easier than not letting his imagination run wild through the lengthy and often involved explanations.

Ben drove to the field. He planned to do a few rounds before leaving Jim for the night. Jim was glad for the company. On the way there, Jim rode on the wheel cover over the back tire of the tractor just as he had seen Mark do before he left. Jim had ridden here before. It was not watching Ben and Mark ride together that had stirred his envy but rather their obvious enjoyment and the man-to-man exchange they'd shared. Jim usually rode in silence, but tonight Mary's question made him bold. It hung in his head, demanding an answer. He was starting a man's job and anxious for comfort before being left with his thoughts for the night.

Jim plunged in. "Dad, I'm sorry Mark's gone."

"Yep, we're going to miss him," Ben mused and then laughed, adding, "We're already missing him!" Then he fell quiet, letting the silence stretch between them.

Disappointed, Jim tried again. "I'm not sorry about the work; I'm glad I get to bale hay. What I'm sorry about is different."

"What do you mean?"

"Somehow we'll get the work done. It's the other part that bothers me," Jim said, feeling his way.

His dad's head came up. "What other part?"

"Well, we can't work the dream without him," Jim said, his frustration spilling out. "You know those things we've talked about, filling in the gullies, improving the land so we have money to build the new house and buy the big tractor we need. We can't do that without Mark to help bring our production up."

His dad was surprised at the conversation. "No, we probably can't," he conceded.

"That's what I'm disappointed about," Jim declared. "It doesn't seem fair that, after all the work we've done together, the dream won't happen, just when we're at the point that it could!"

Ben was quiet.

Through the light from the tractor, Jim watched his dad blinking and swallowing hard and felt anxious, fearing he had said too much. They drove in silence for several minutes and had reached the hay field and pulled into position beside the windrow before his dad spoke again.

"The new house and the tractor, that's just part of the dream," Ben said. "There's a piece of the dream you've been too young to understand."

"What piece is that?" Jim asked.

"The piece where you look around the farm and ask, 'Do I want to do this for the rest of my life? Is my dream here?' If it is, that's great; you'd be a terrific partner. If it isn't, the farm has still been a success. You know how to work and take responsibility. You have the skills to build your own dream."

Now Jim was quiet. He had never supposed that his dad felt that way or that he would extend that kind of personal license. As Ben's words flowed through him, the resentment that had festered in him for weeks over Mark's leaving, burst. He felt liberated, free, happy, light, and giddy. He felt like bursting into song and then leaping from the tractor and racing it through the hayfield. In the end, he didn't do any of that; he just held tightly to the tractor mount and looked into his dad's beaming face.

Despite the perils and aggravations of baling hay at night, in the morning rows and rows of neat rectangular packages laced the field. Jim was proud of his work. The night had passed more quickly than he had supposed. Through the endless ups and downs of the field, his mind had wandered freely, pondering the offer. What did he want to do? What was his dream? Was it here?

***

My dad was a dream-builder; he taught us how to put a foundation under our dreams. We worked together every summer day on a farm that he let us feel we owned. Each of us became independent-minded, demanding about the amount of work to be done, what the finished job should look like, and the dedication our tasks required. Our daily work brought us to depend on each other, trust each other, and even cuss each other as we tried to make Dad's success our success. After all, we thought, we owned the place.

The dream we pursued really belonged to our parents. Time would show that, in spite of our determination to posses it, when Dad retired, talent and interests would make other choices for all of us. None of us chose to pursue farming as our dream. But in our glorious youth we were sure the land would always be ours. In the end, our dream was not his dream, but Dad cut us loose, smiled his broad smile and applauded each of us as we wobbled forth.

Money Wrapped in a Dream

Author's Note & Discussion Questions

Our childhood lives within us always.

1. In the end, what did Ben and Ruth end up giving their children?

2. What role did money play in the execution of this family's dreams?

3. If they had had lots of money, would that have helped or hindered them?

Afterword

A Celebration Story

> *Not all dreams are the same. Some are better than others. One test of a dream is what we see spring from it into the hearts of the next generation.*
>
> -Lucy Beutler

A delivery truck whined to a stop in front of the house, and multiple thuds on the driveway announced the arrival of the Christmas edition of the newspaper. I eased my eyes open and stretched to wakefulness. The dial on the alarm clock read 4:50 a.m. The night had already been interrupted with Santa work, and my husband and I had retired to bed just two hours earlier, leaving the shades up to enjoy the glow of Christmas lights shimmering through the windows. Now the un-shaded windows revealed that fresh snow was falling outside. It would be a white Christmas!

Full of excitement, I snuggled next to my sleeping husband to savor the joy of it, but the bundles stacked by the garage door were hard to ignore. Like a living presence, they were demanding attention, waiting for human hands to invite them out of the cold and begin the long process that would insure their delivery.

From years of experience, I knew that the Christmas edition of the paper would be massive. It was only outdone in size by the one on Thanksgiving Day. All the merchants would either be announcing a sale or running an ad to express appreciation to their customers. Our children felt the paper should be cancelled. The idea of someone waiting for a newspaper on Christmas morning seemed incredible to them. But they had learned, through hard experience, that there were always those who waited. Still, the idea of waking anyone to *deliver* those papers on Christmas morning seemed cruel. But there was no reason to lie in bed and chafe over it. We needed the money from the paper routes to sustain our family. At least this year the papers were on time and not hours late, like they had been last year. If everyone helped, we could get them folded and delivered and be home again by 7 a.m. to begin our own festivities.

Sensing that I was awake, my husband stirred beside me. "Paper's here," he mumbled.

"Uh huh," I mumbled back, "and it's snowing!"

He turned over, wrapping his arms around me and adjusting our pillows so we could both watch the white flakes hurdle from the sky. We stayed like that for several minutes before he said, "Best get going. You stay in bed. I'll get up and start the papers."

"I'll help," I protested. "Then the children can rest longer."

"You stay in bed for an hour and then start breakfast. I'll wake the kids when I need them. It's my gift to you."

Sensing my objection, he whispered into my hair. "The snow and an extra hour in bed will be all you get for Christmas this year. Enjoy your gift." He kissed me, crawled from bed, and began to dress.

I knew he was right. There wasn't a package from him under the Christmas tree this year. This was my gift. I burrowed into the covers to enjoy it. To say that things were tight was an understatement. My husband didn't worry much about Christmas; I wished I could be as calm. It had taken imagination, burning the midnight oil, and lots of cutting back from both of us to put a package under the tree for each of our children this year.

It was 1985. Four years earlier we had moved across the country, enticed by an employment opportunity, a job my husband had dreamed of. He loved his work and was glad we had made the decision to come. But just before the move, double-digit interest rates had spawned a downturn in the housing market that made it difficult for us to sell our properties. Our home finally sold, but despite having made major improvements on it, it sold without profit. Our new home was smaller than the one we'd left behind, but the high interest rates tripled our mortgage payment. Along with that, we had been unsuccessful in finding a buyer for our rental property. Under our management the unit had paid for itself and put money in the bank. But under the management of a third party, instead of a positive return each month we received bills that crippled our household budget.

As I watched my husband find his clothes in the dark and dress in the shadows, I felt comforted by his goodness. Where did he find the energy to serve us? He never slept in, even on Christmas.

Two years ago one of our neighbors had grown tired of his paper route and offered it to our children. Delivering 100 papers, seven days a week, was a big job, but our two oldest sons were enthusiastic. The route required front-door delivery before 7 a.m. on weekends and holidays and before 6 p.m. on weekdays. Not only was delivery required, but the carriers were expected to contact each customer monthly to collect payment as well. The constraint of our budget made our sons eager for the work. The paper route would help them meet some of their own expenses and have a little pocket money as well. The plan worked perfectly in the summer. When one of our sons was gone, the other would cover. On weekends when both of them were gone, my husband delivered. When they were all at scout camp, I delivered, with our toddler on the back of my bicycle and the paper bags on the front.

The challenge came in the fall when both of the older boys made school basketball teams. After-school basketball practice made it impossible for them to deliver all the papers. The rub was that they needed the money from the paper routes to be on the team. It was expensive to travel with the team and pay for practice fees and uniforms. We couldn't help from the family budget. The answer came when our daughter, who was ten, and our son, who was seven, volunteered to fold and bag all the papers after school each day as well as deliver the 50 papers that were closest to our home. With the papers folded and bagged, our older sons could deliver the papers that were farther away after practice.

Weekday games presented another dilemma. On those days we had to deliver all the papers. Neither of our older sons could come home from school to help out, and my husband couldn't come from work. To make things worse, it was winter—snowy and icy and dark. I didn't feel good about the kids going so far from home to deliver the papers. Taking them in the car only complicated the delivery. It was much faster on bikes. Game days I went with them, my toddler in his snowsuit on the back of my bike and a bag of papers on the front. Those were epic adventures.

I could hear my husband's voice in the hallway waking our sons to help with the papers. Sounds of them toppling out of bed and jockeying for position to get the first look under the Christmas tree delighted me. Even papers couldn't dampen their excitement for Christmas. Finally he herded them into the garage. I smiled as I heard his activity. There wasn't a present under the tree for him today either, but he was getting a gift too. He didn't know about it, but I hoped he would love it.

My hour was over. If breakfast was to be ready when they returned, I'd better get up. Reluctant to leave the warmth of the covers, I watched the falling snow for another minute before rolling out. On the way to the kitchen I stood in the doorway of the family room and looked at the tree standing majestically in the corner. Last night, after we had set out the gifts, I had straightened the room, anticipating this very moment. The tree was lovely, with the lights playing off the deep red and gold of the ornaments and the presents peeping out from under the tips of the branches. It was usually one of my favorite Christmas moments, but this year it made my stomach knot. It was still so obvious. Even though I had spaced the presents farther apart and wrapped our traditional boxes of cereal and crackers so there were more packages under the tree, it still looked like there was almost nothing. My husband was better at dealing with scarcity than I was. I should be glad for what was there, but my heart was afraid our children would be disappointed. We had great kids. I wanted to give each of them a nice gift, something they had dreamed about.

Some wrapping paper under the chair by the tree caught my attention. Surprised at it, I walked over, knelt down and reached between the legs of the chair to pick it up. But it wasn't a scrap; two large packages had been stuffed under the skirt of the chair. The knot in my stomach began to relax. The other Santa had already come.

Money Wrapped in a Dream

It had happened in October. School was out, and it was chilly in the garage as I helped the kids take the security bands off the advertisements so they could collate them into the papers.

"Mom," my daughter said, "the boys both need a new coat for Christmas."

"You're right, they do," I responded. "But they'll have to wait until next year. We don't have money for coats this year." My answer was automatic and truthful. I had gotten used to saying it.

"But Mom, they really need them. The sleeves are way up on their arms," she persisted.

"I know, but they'll have to get by; all of us will. We have other priorities this year."

"The team wears really nice coats. I've seen them," she persisted.

Not to be outdone, her younger brother piped in, "They're freezing. They don't even take their coats."

"That's their choice," I responded.

"How much would it cost for a new coat?" she asked.

"More than we have," I said and walked into the house, wanting to end the discussion.

To my surprise, two weeks later the discussion had begun again. In the circulars the children were collating into the newspapers was an advertisement from one of the department stores for a coat sale. The coats were pictured in full color, and the kids wanted my opinion. Would this be a good coat for their brothers? Was it a good buy? Did I think another one would be better?

I dreaded having this conversation again. They were right. Their older brothers did need new coats, but nothing had changed about our finances. There wasn't any way to work the numbers and make the scarcity go away. It seemed cruel to squash their hopes.

I almost choked on the words. "Even on sale we can't afford the coats."

"I know, Mom," my daughter said, "but if you think they're good ones, *we'll* buy them."

"What do you mean, you'll buy them?"

"We'll use the money in our savings," she said. "He'll buy one and I'll buy the other," she said, indicating her little brother as she spoke.

"But you're both saving for something else," I protested. Though they managed and delivered the paper route, the money from the route went to their brothers, except for $15 a month they each put in savings.

"We were; but the coats won't take all of it. The boys need them. That's more important right now."

Their goodness had freed my heart, and tears had streamed from my eyes, running down my face and onto my shirt. Despite genuine personal needs, they were placing those of their brothers first. Joy filled my whole being. It was a swelling gladness. I had experienced this joy before. It had been years ago on my first date with my husband, when I had glimpsed the goodness of his heart. Our children had chosen to sacrifice and do something extremely good, and I had glimpsed their hearts. I had seen the dream leap to the next generation.

My children were confused, and a little embarrassed, at my emotion. I couldn't stop crying, nor could I really explain to them what I was weeping over. I just kept telling them, "I'm proud of you." And I was.

We'd had a glorious time at the department store looking at the coats. The kids wanted to see them all. In the end, they chose coats in team colors, like the ones the boys' teammates wore. The clerk had rung up the ticket and held the coats for us while we went to the credit union and withdrew my children's money. I had helped them wrap the boxes last night but had not seen them stuff the gifts under the chair for Santa to bring. Though the coats had been purchased almost two months ago, we had shared the secret with no one; I had not even shared it with my husband. He knew nothing of the celebration in the garage that day months ago. He would find out today. It was to be his gift.

I walked to the kitchen to begin breakfast, my heart suddenly light. I had gone to bed worried last night, knowing Christmas was small this year, lamenting the limited number of packages under the tree. But I had been mistaken. Could Christmas be much bigger than this?

Money Wrapped in a Dream
Author's Note & Discussion Question

Families have a foundational duty to pass to the next generation basic values that enable their children and grandchildren to make a "good life." Building a dream requires children to sacrifice self-interest, to be trustworthy, and to work together. Financial tight spots provide natural learning opportunities for them.

Looking back on this experience, I realize that if I could have, I would have changed things and, in so doing, robbed my children of the very circumstances that were schooling them. We can stretch our children too little or push them too hard.

1. What happened in the story that allowed the sacrifice required by the paper route to build character and well being?

Postscript I
Map of the Farm

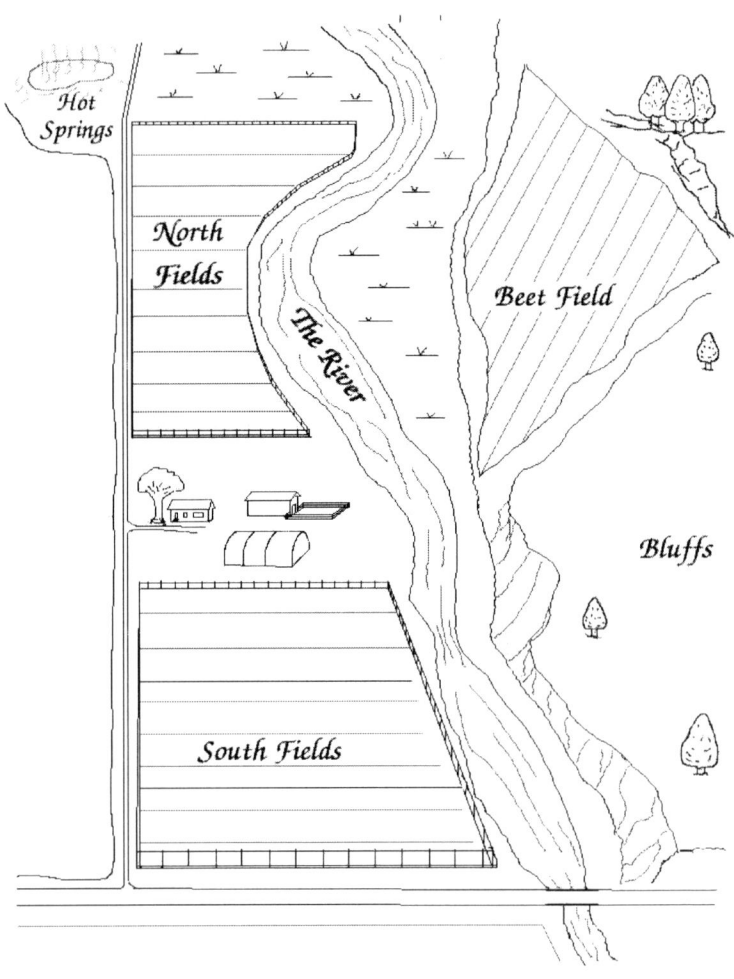

Postscript II
Who's Who in the Family

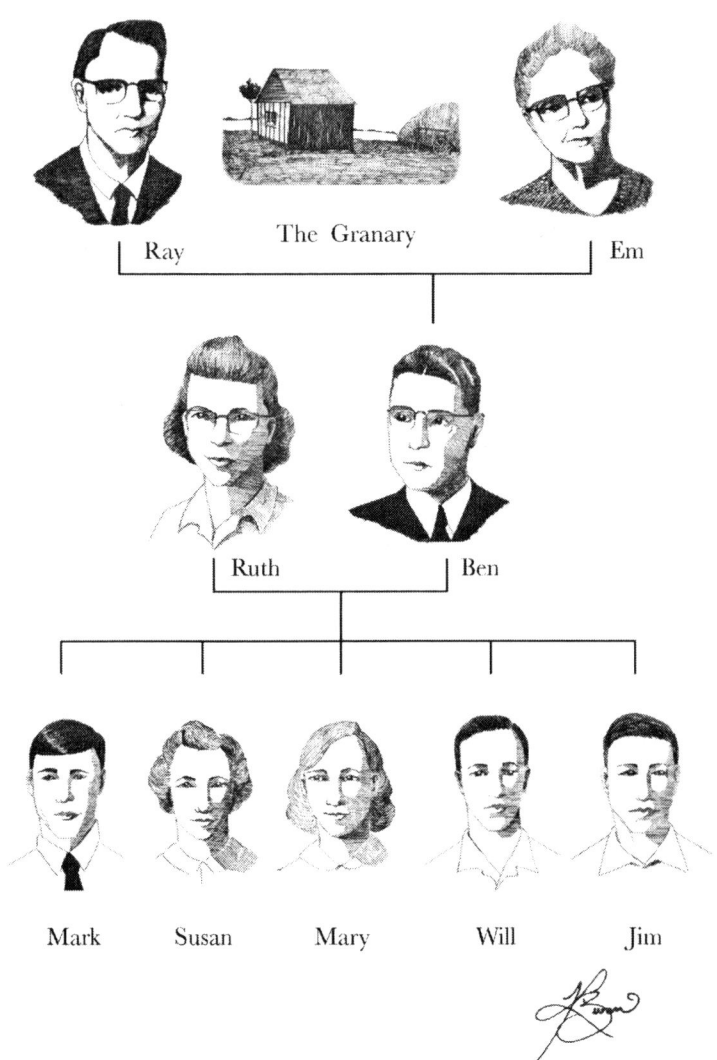

Want to know more?

Join the conversation at www.harringtongates.com

About HarringtonGates

HarringtonGates was created to encourage research on money and the family. Our aim is to address a central question that has been long neglected: how may money be earned and then used in ways that help produce an effective and joyful home?

Conventional discussions of personal finance assume that more is better than less—that the person with the most stuff wins—that to lose all you own is to lose it all. As a result, many of the conclusions in personal finance, while helpful, have limited application.

The work at HarringtonGates assumes that money is not the end but rather an important means that enables family activities and functions. Families have a foundational duty to pass to the next generation basic values that enable their children and grandchildren to make a "good life." Building a successful dream requires parents and children to sacrifice self-interest and work together to acquire and utilize financial resources.

Here is a sample of topics HarringtonGates addresses:

- Reaching your highest potential at work
- Keeping well-balanced harmony between work and home
- Getting both husband and wife on the same page
- Making better financial decisions by counseling together
- Teaching children to contribute to the total family welfare
- Giving in ways that empower others
- Spending money effectively and powerfully
- Flourishing despite adversity

For more information, go to www.harringtongates.com.